REVIVING
—OUR—
REPUBLIC

www.reviveourrepublic.com

ISBN: 979-8-9914226-0-4 (paperback)
ISBN: 979-8-9914226-1-1 (ebook)
ISBN: 979-8-9914226-2-8 (hardcover)
ISBN: 979-8-9914226-3-5 (audiobook)

Ordering Information:
Special discounts are available on quantity purchases by corporations, associations, and others. For details, contact www.reviveourrepublic.com

REVIVING
— OUR —
REPUBLIC

95 THESES
FOR THE FUTURE
OF AMERICA

A CITIZEN'S CALL FOR
RESTORING OUR
NATION'S PRINCIPLES

WRITTEN BY
MIKE BEDENBAUGH

Dedicated to Carson, Jacob, Amanda, Lilith, Maggie,
Lauren, Nick, Michelle, and Renee.
For they, and their children, will reap tomorrow
what we sow today.

This is the true joy in life, being used for a purpose recognized by yourself as a mighty one. Being a force of nature instead of a feverish, selfish little clod of ailments and grievances, complaining that the world will not devote itself to making you happy. I am of the opinion that my life belongs to the whole community and as long as I live, it is my privilege to do for it what I can. I want to be thoroughly used up when I die, for the harder I work, the more I live. I rejoice in life for its own sake. Life is no brief candle to me. It is a sort of splendid torch which I have got hold of for the moment and I want to make it burn as brightly as possible before handing it on to future generations.

—George Bernard Shaw

TABLE OF CONTENTS

INTRODUCTION

THE INSPIRATION FOR THE PREMISE of this book began on the night of August 6, 2015, when I witnessed the first national Republican debate for the 2016 presidential campaign. On the stage were the leading Republicans in the country vying for the post-Obama White House: Jeb Bush, Scott Walker, Mike Huckabee, Ben Carson, Ted Cruz, Marco Rubio, Rand Paul, Chris Christie, John Kasich, and Donald Trump. By the time that debate was over, I knew the world of American politics would never be the same.

In July prior to the debate, during a trip to Washington, DC, I had the opportunity to visit Mount Vernon. While there, I purchased a biography of George Washington by Ron Chernow. I had just finished reading its 900 pages when I sat in my darkened living room that evening and allowed the reality to sink in that our politics had finally achieved the ultimate conclusion of a wealthy, consumptive society; instead of a knowledgeable debate that elevated solutions to big problems, it was now just another toxic spectator sport.

Reflecting on the debates and the biography, I found myself drawn to another book that had profoundly influenced Washington, *The Book of Virtues*. Washington's moral compass and steadfast character, which guided him through the American Revolution and his presidency, were shaped by the virtues extolled in this book. As I juxtaposed the dignified, principled leadership of Washington with the brash, combative nature of the debate, I realized that what I was witnessing was exactly what he had feared might happen when Americans forgot the lessons Washington shared with our ancestors over 230 years before.

But why is George Washington still important to us now? With all the problems facing the United States of America in the 21st century, why would we look for inspiration from a wealthy and privileged white slaveholder from the 18th century? His faults regarding slavery are clear, and his inability to publicly face the hypocrisy of forging a new nation that could ensure liberty for "all" built on the backs of chattel slavery casts a dark shadow on his record of leadership. We cannot disregard his 18th-century outlook regarding social classes and racial prejudice.

We also cannot disregard his ability to lead and inspire others to build a new national government that would work and be acceptable to the states. The men who met in Philadelphia during the hot summer of 1787 were not founders of a new society as much as they were architects, utilizing their vast knowledge, applying it to the social landscape that existed at the time, and constructing an edifice unlike any ever constructed. However, everyone in the room knew that there was only one man alive who could lead such an intellectual and political rabble, and they appointed him chairman of the convention. To put it bluntly, without George Washington's example of leadership during the American Revolution and as president of the Constitutional Convention, our nation would not exist.

As the preeminent revolutionary leader, he ensured that the unity among the revolutionary generation, forged by a common purpose of war and nationhood, would not be destroyed during the infancy of our republic's formation. Only George Washington could hold together the Continental Army long enough to defeat the British will to fight, persuade his army officers involved in the Newburgh Conspiracy against overthrowing the elected leadership of the Congress, take the leadership chair of the Constitutional Convention, and become our first president and model for presidents to follow. All these things were able to take place because he understood more than anyone the importance of words and the symbolism needed for a successful republic to exist.

Throughout history, many "successful" revolutions in various societies have often devolved into civil war among their instigators. However, it was George Washington's exemplary leadership and strength of character that forged a unifying principle so robust that our inevitable civil war was delayed for four score and seven years. This delay, until the grandchildren of the founding generation were in power, provided sufficient time for the Constitution to establish its legitimacy as our governing document, ensuring its endurance through the conflagration of 1861.

As chief architect, he knew full well that the structure they created in Philadelphia was going to require a "maintenance plan" so it could stay strong and stable. That maintenance plan was published before he voluntarily retired from the presidency. We know it today as his Farewell Address.

I am convinced that the terrible state we are in now is a direct result of our ignoring the maintenance manual Washington left us. Just as Martin Luther nailed his 95 Theses to the church door in Wittenberg to protest the corruption of the 16th-century Catholic Church and spark the Reformation, I envision my theses as a catalyst for conversation about a new kind of reform against what many see as a corrupted republic. Many of these theses cannot be promulgated overnight and will take time to build a national consensus to enact. Through this book, I hope to inspire a national discussion and revival of the spirit of intentional citizenship that animated the founding of the United States.

Over the past decade, I have utilized the phrase "Place, Purpose, and Preservation" as a sign-off on my podcast and You Tube channel "Perspective with Mike Bedenbaugh" to promote the historic preservation of a specific historic site and the community in which it was located. However, with the writing of this book, that phrase now encompasses a broader scope, including local community, state, and national government that encapsulates the foundational pillars essential to maintaining the integrity of our nation's republic.

"Place" refers to the environments and settings that shape our individual identities, emphasizing how our connection to specific locations and communities helps define who we are as citizens and lays the groundwork for our personal and collective sense of belonging.

"Purpose" underscores our responsibility as citizens to defend the guiding principles and values enshrined in the Constitution, such as liberty, justice, and democracy, which serve as the moral compass directing our collective actions and governance.

"Preservation" highlights the need for vigilant safeguarding of both our physical and natural heritage as well as core principles to ensure that future generations inherit a nation that remains true to its ideals.

Together, these elements stress the vital role of maintaining a strong connection to our past, upholding our democratic values, and actively working to protect the legacy of the republic for posterity.

PREAMBLE

Out of love for Country and Liberty, and the desire to ensure the elevation of solutions for its survival, I present the following propositions to be discussed and defended in town halls, county seats, state capitals, and Washington, DC with the expectation of correcting the indulgences of our nation's political and corporate leadership.

The theses posted in this book were created in hopes to moderate the fury of party spirit, to warn against the mischiefs of foreign intrigue, to guard against the impostures of pretended patriotism, to disempower global corporate hegemony, and to offer structural mechanisms to mitigate their excesses so as to empower individual liberty of…we the people.

THESIS 1

The United States of America was created by citizens of many cultures and religious creeds whose leadership was elected to ensure self-governance for the people.

THESIS 2

Self-governance requires a legitimate basis for the creation of laws that protect the rights of an independent citizenry.

THESIS 3

*The United States required a framework of governance for the
establishment of legitimacy in its laws.*

THESIS 4

*The citizens who created that original framework of our government
should be considered architects who constructed a foundation on which
to build a new legitimate system of governance.*

THESIS 5

*The citizen architects of our system of governance constructed the
foundational principles to house the aspirations of many people under
one roof in order to create one nation.*

THESIS 6

*The architects of this nation were the most politically knowledgeable
men of their day, but with social perspectives limited to their
time and place.*

THESIS 7

*The architects of this nation, understanding moral fallibility is inherent
in humans seeking power, created a structure of checks and balances to
limit the inevitable damage that can occur when centralized power to
alter that structure is left unchecked.*

THESIS 8

*The architects of this nation, understanding the limitations in their
own social perspectives, created a structure that can be renovated
(amended) by the citizens within a prescribed rule of law.*

THESIS 9

The chief architect and first president of this governmental structure, George Washington, delivered to the people of this nation an owner's manual, or guide, in the form of a farewell address on how future generations could best maintain the structure.

THESIS 10

Our first president's guide to governance warns of the dangers to our government structure that were recognized in 18th-century America if parasitic influences and neglect of duty are left unchecked and unchallenged.

THESIS 11

Since the publication of the owner's manual 227 years ago, generations have grown numb to the potential dangers of these pitfalls.

THESIS 12

Our cumulative lack of disciplined diligence to our owner's manual has created a governmental structure that has been undermined by the cumulative and generational laziness of citizens who have allowed an opportunistic and parasitic politicized leadership who gain prominence and power through discord and division.

THESIS 13

The primary points of Washington's owner's manual can be divided into four themes:

- Moderating the fury of party spirit
- Warning against the mischiefs of foreign intrigue
- Guarding against the impostures of pretended patriotism
- Maintaining fiscal responsibility

Part I

❖

WASHINGTON'S REFLECTIONS ON PARTY SPIRIT AND FEIGNED PATRIOTISM

Patriotism means to stand by the country. It does not mean to stand by the president or any other public official.

—THEODORE ROOSEVELT

CENTRAL TO WASHINGTON'S VISION FOR a unified and prosperous republic were his profound insights into the perils of partisan discord and the dangers of superficial displays of patriotism. In this chapter, I take inspiration from Washington's thoughts on party spirit and feigned patriotism which are encapsulated in theses 14–21. It is an incredible legacy to his political foresight when we reflect on how, after over two centuries, their relevance still endures in today's political landscape.

THESIS 14

This spirit of party is inseparable from our nature, but, in those governments of the popular form, it is truly their worst enemy.

THESIS 15

The alternate domination of one faction over another, sharpened by the spirit of revenge, is a frightful despotism.

George Washington's warning about the dangers of partisan politics and the spirit of revenge is reflected in numerous historical examples around the world where factionalism and party spirit have undermined the functioning of popular governments. Here are some notable instances:

Ancient Rome: The conflict between the Populares (leaders who sought the support of the common people) and the Optimates (aristocratic leaders) led to severe political instability. The rivalry between Julius Caesar and Pompey, both representing different factions, eventually culminated in a civil war, contributing to the end of the Roman Republic and the rise of the Roman Empire.

The English Civil War (1642–1651): The war was fueled by intense factionalism between the Royalists (supporters of King Charles I) and the Parliamentarians (supporters of the parliamentary system). This conflict led to a temporary overthrow of the monarchy and the establishment of the Commonwealth under Oliver Cromwell. The strife and division during this period significantly weakened England and led to the eventual restoration of the monarchy in 1660.

The French Revolution (1789–1799): The revolution saw intense factionalism, particularly between the Girondins and the Jacobins. This internal strife led to the Reign of Terror, where thousands were executed, including many former revolutionaries. The instability and violence of this period paved the way for Napoleon Bonaparte's rise to power and the establishment of a more autocratic regime.

The Revolutions of 1848 in Europe: Known as the "Springtime of Nations," these revolutions were marked by widespread revolutionary movements across Europe, including in France, Germany, Italy, and the Austrian Empire. The revolutions were often driven by conflicting political ideologies and factional interests, leading to significant political upheaval and, in many cases, the reestablishment of conservative regimes after initial successes by the revolutionaries.

Weimar Republic (Germany, 1919–1933): The Weimar Republic faced severe political fragmentation with numerous parties across the political spectrum, from the far-left Communists to the far-right Nazis. This fragmentation and the inability to form stable governments contributed to political paralysis, economic crises, and eventually, the rise of Adolf Hitler and the Nazi Party.

Post-Independence India (1947 onwards): India has experienced significant political factionalism, particularly in states with strong regional parties. In states like Tamil Nadu, the rivalry between major regional parties such as the AIADMK and DMK has often led to political instability and governance challenges. This factionalism has sometimes hampered economic development and effective governance.

Nigeria (1960s onwards): Nigeria has experienced significant political factionalism, often along ethnic and regional lines. The First Republic (1963–1966) saw intense rivalry between political parties representing different ethnic groups. This factionalism contributed to a series of military coups and a devastating civil war (1967–1970), significantly destabilizing the country.

Chile (1970s): The election of Salvador Allende, a socialist, in 1970 led to significant polarization in Chilean society. The intense opposition from right-wing parties and sectors of the military, coupled with economic challenges, culminated in a military coup in 1973, led by General Augusto Pinochet. This coup ended Chile's democracy and resulted in a brutal military dictatorship lasting until 1990.

United States (Civil War Era, 1860s): The intense sectionalism and party spirit between the Northern and Southern states, primarily over the issue of slavery, led to the Civil War. This conflict resulted in immense loss of life and significant damage to the country's political and social fabric.

THESIS 16

The disorders and miseries which result gradually incline the minds of men to seek security and repose in the power of an individual.

THESIS 17

Sooner or later the chief of some prevailing faction…turns this disposition to the purposes of their own elevation.

George Washington's observations on governance were informed by his extensive knowledge of history, especially the example of the Roman Republic's transformation into a tyrannical empire. Additionally, the English Civil War, which had occurred in the relatively recent century before his birth, also influenced his perspective. His warning about how societal disorders and miseries can lead people to seek security in the power of an individual has been reflected throughout history and has proven to be timeless in that we unfortunately have numerous examples that occurred after his passing.

Ancient Rome: The political chaos and social unrest during the late Roman Republic led many Romans to seek stability in strong leadership. This environment allowed Julius Caesar to gain extraordinary power and ultimately become dictator for life. After his assassination, Augustus (formerly Octavian) emerged from the ensuing power struggles and established himself as the first Roman Emperor, marking the end of the Republic and the beginning of the Roman Empire.

The English Civil War (1642–1651): The war was fueled by intense factionalism between the Royalists (supporters of King Charles I) and the Parliamentarians (supporters of the parliamentary system). This conflict led to a temporary overthrow of the monarchy and the establishment of the Commonwealth under Oliver Cromwell. The strife and division during this period significantly weakened England and led to the eventual restoration of the monarchy in 1660.

The French Revolution (1789–1799): The revolution saw intense factionalism, particularly between the Girondins and the Jacobins. This internal strife led to the Reign of Terror, where thousands were executed, including many former revolutionaries. The instability and violence of this period paved the way for Napoleon Bonaparte's rise to power, first as First Consul and then as Emperor, establishing a dictatorial regime that promised order and security.

The Revolutions of 1848 in Europe: Known as the "Springtime of Nations," these revolutions were marked by widespread revolutionary movements across Europe, including in France, Germany, Italy, and the Austrian Empire. The revolutions were often driven by conflicting political ideologies and factional interests, leading to significant political upheaval and, in many cases, the re-establishment of conservative regimes after initial successes by the revolutionaries.

Weimar Germany (1919–1933): The Weimar Republic faced severe economic hardship, political instability, and social unrest. Hyperinflation, unemployment, and fear of communism drove many Germans to seek a strong leader who could restore order and national pride. This environment facilitated Adolf Hitler's rise to power, leading to his establishment of a totalitarian regime.

Spain (1930s): The political instability and social unrest during the Second Spanish Republic (1931–1939) culminated in the Spanish Civil War (1936–1939). The conflict was marked by intense factionalism and violence. Following the Nationalist victory, many Spaniards, weary of the chaos, supported Francisco Franco, who established a military dictatorship. Franco's regime promised order and stability, and he ruled Spain with an iron fist until his death in 1975.

Vietnam (1940s–1970s): Following the end of French colonial rule, Vietnam experienced significant turmoil, including the First Indochina War and the division of the country into North and South Vietnam. The disorders and hardships of continuous conflict inclined many Vietnamese to support strong leaders. In the North, Ho Chi Minh emerged as the leader of the Democratic Republic of Vietnam, establishing a communist regime. In the South, Ngo Dinh Diem's authoritarian rule was initially supported by many as a bulwark against communism, though his oppressive policies eventually led to his downfall.

Cambodia (1970s): The instability and conflict during the Cambodian Civil War (1967–1975), coupled with the bombings and spillover effects of the Vietnam War, created immense suffering and chaos in Cambodia. In this context, the Khmer Rouge, led by Pol Pot, seized power in 1975. Pol Pot established a brutal regime that promised to create a classless agrarian society but resulted in the deaths of an estimated 1.7 to 2 million people through forced labor, starvation, and executions.

Philippines (1970s–1980s): Following a period of political unrest and economic difficulties, President Ferdinand Marcos declared martial law in 1972. This move was initially supported by many Filipinos who desired stability and order. Marcos's regime promised to combat corruption and economic challenges but eventually became known for its authoritarian rule, human rights abuses, and corruption. He remained in power until the People Power Revolution of 1986, which led to his ouster.

Russia (Post-1917 Revolution): After the Russian Revolution and the subsequent civil war, Russia was plunged into chaos and suffering. The disorders and miseries of this period made many Russians yearn for stability and security.

This desire was a significant factor in the Bolsheviks' consolidation of power under Vladimir Lenin and later Joseph Stalin, who established a dictatorial regime with tight control over the state.

Chile (1970s): The economic difficulties, political polarization, and social unrest during Salvador Allende's presidency led many Chileans to desire a return to order. This situation contributed to the military coup led by General Augusto Pinochet in 1973. Pinochet established a military dictatorship that promised stability and economic reform, though it was also marked by severe repression and human rights abuses.

China (1940s–1950s): Following decades of warlordism, Japanese invasion, and civil war, China was in a state of disarray. The Chinese people, exhausted by the continuous strife, increasingly looked to the Chinese Communist Party and Mao Zedong for stability. Mao's rise to power and the establishment of the People's Republic of China led to a centralized, authoritarian regime promising order and progress, though it also brought about significant turmoil and hardship through policies like the Great Leap Forward and the Cultural Revolution.

THESIS 18

The spirit of passionate factionalism always serves to distract the public councils and enfeeble the public administration.

THESIS 19

Factionalism agitates the citizenry with ill-founded jealousy and false alarms.

The quote about the dangers of passionate factionalism highlights how intense political divisions can distract government decision-making, weaken administration, and create public unrest through unfounded fears and misinformation. Here are examples from American history illustrating these points:

THE RED SCARE OF THE 1950S

Context: During the early Cold War, fears of communism spread across the United States, fueled by the Soviet Union's expansion and domestic espionage concerns.

Factionalism: Senator Joseph McCarthy and other anti-communist leaders exploited these fears to root out supposed communists within the government and other institutions. This period, known as McCarthyism, was marked by aggressive investigations and accusations, often without proper evidence.

Impact on Public Councils and Administration: The intense anti-communist sentiment distracted the government from other pressing issues, causing a significant portion of political energy and resources to be diverted toward rooting out perceived internal threats. This led to a chilling effect on free speech and political dissent, as well as a climate of suspicion and paranoia.

Agitation of Citizenry: McCarthyism stirred widespread fear and suspicion among the American public. The constant stream of accusations created an environment of distrust, leading many to believe that communists had infiltrated all levels of American society. This ill-founded jealousy and these false alarms disrupted communities and damaged reputations.

THE KNOW NOTHING PARTY OF THE 1850S

Context: In the mid-19th century, the United States saw significant immigration, particularly from Ireland and Germany. This influx of immigrants sparked nativist sentiments among some Americans.

Factionalism: The Know Nothing Party (officially the American Party) emerged as a political movement dedicated to curbing immigration and opposing the influence of Catholics. The party's platform was built on xenophobia and anti-Catholic rhetoric.

Impact on Public Councils and Administration: The rise of the Know Nothing Party distracted public councils by focusing political debate on issues of ethnicity and culture of immigrants and religion. Their influence led to legislative efforts to restrict the rights of immigrants and limit their political power.

Agitation of Citizenry: The Know Nothing Party's rhetoric and policies incited fear and hostility toward immigrants, particularly Catholics. This created social divisions and unrest, as nativist propaganda spread false alarms about the supposed threat immigrants posed to American values and institutions. These sentiments contributed to societal tension and violence, including riots and clashes between native-born citizens and immigrant communities.

Washington's warning underscores the divisive impact of partisan rhetoric on societal cohesion. When citizens are misled by exaggerated grievances, it can elevate fear to a level where social unity is compromised, paving the way for further polarization.

THESIS 20

Factionalism kindles the animosity of one group against another in ways that can occasionally foment riot and insurrection.

THE NEW YORK DRAFT RIOTS (1863)

Context: During the Civil War, the Union instituted a draft to bolster its forces, allowing wealthier men to pay for substitutes to take their place. This policy incited outrage among the working class, particularly Irish immigrants.

Factionalism: Tensions between Irish immigrants and free African Americans, coupled with anger toward the wealthy who could avoid the draft, created a volatile mix. Political factionalism also played a role, as many Irish immigrants were Democrats opposed to the Republican-led war effort.

Riot: The draft riots erupted in July 1863, lasting several days. Rioters targeted African Americans, Republican supporters, and symbols of wealth, leading to widespread violence, destruction, and deaths. The riots were eventually quelled by federal troops, but not before substantial damage had been done.

THE TULSA RACE MASSACRE (1921)

Context: In Tulsa, Oklahoma, the prosperous African American neighborhood of Greenwood, known as "Black Wall Street," existed alongside a predominantly white community.

Factionalism: Racial tensions, exacerbated by economic envy and segregationist attitudes, were stoked by false allegations against a Black man accused of assaulting a white woman.

Riot: In May 1921, white mobs attacked Greenwood, burning homes and businesses, and killing an estimated 100 to 300 African Americans. The violence left thousands homeless and destroyed one of the most affluent Black communities in the United States.

THE DETROIT RACE RIOT (1943)

Context: During World War II, Detroit experienced a massive influx of workers, including African Americans migrating from the South, leading to housing shortages and job competition.

Factionalism: Racial tensions between Black and white residents, fueled by competition for jobs and housing, as well as resentment over perceived privileges.

Riot: In June 1943, a fight between Black and white youths at Belle Isle Park escalated into a citywide riot. For several days, violence ensued, with both

Black and white rioters attacking each other and property. Federal troops were deployed to restore order, but the riots resulted in 34 deaths and extensive property damage.

THE WATTS RIOTS (1965)

Context: The Watts neighborhood of Los Angeles was predominantly African American, with significant issues of poverty, unemployment, and police brutality as perceived by the Black residents.

Factionalism: Long-standing racial tensions and allegations of police misconduct against African Americans fueled resentment and anger.

Riot: In August 1965, a traffic stop involving a Black motorist escalated into a confrontation, sparking six days of rioting. The violence resulted in 34 deaths, over 1,000 injuries, and significant destruction of property. The National Guard was called in to restore order.

THE CHICAGO RIOT (1968)

Context: In the context of the Civil Rights Movement and opposition to the Vietnam War, tensions were high in many American cities. The assassination of Dr. Martin Luther King Jr. further inflamed these tensions.

Factionalism: The division between civil rights activists, anti-war protestors, and the political establishment was pronounced. Racial tensions also contributed to the unrest.

Riot: Following King's assassination in April 1968, riots erupted in several cities, including Chicago. In Chicago, the violence lasted for several days, with significant destruction in predominantly African American neighborhoods. The National Guard and federal troops were deployed to quell the riots.

THE LOS ANGELES RIOTS (1992)

Context: The acquittal of four Los Angeles police officers charged with the beating of Rodney King, an African American motorist, led to widespread outrage and disbelief, particularly in the African American community.

Factionalism: Racial tensions between African American residents and the predominantly white police force, along with economic disparities and previous instances of police brutality, created a highly charged atmosphere.

Riot: In April 1992, following the acquittal, riots broke out in Los Angeles. Over six days, the city experienced extensive violence, arson, looting, and clashes with law enforcement. The riots resulted in 63 deaths, thousands of injuries, and significant property damage, requiring the deployment of the National Guard and federal troops.

THE MINNEAPOLIS RIOTS (2020)

Context: The murder of George Floyd, an African American man, by a white police officer in Minneapolis sparked nationwide protests against police brutality and systemic racism.

Factionalism: Long-standing racial tensions, coupled with incidents of police violence against African Americans, led to widespread outrage. Political polarization and social media also played roles in mobilizing protestors.

Riot: In May 2020, protests in Minneapolis quickly escalated into riots, with significant property damage, including the burning of a police precinct. The unrest spread to cities across the United States, leading to a national reckoning on race relations and police reform.

THE CAPITOL RIOT (JANUARY 6, 2021)

Context: In the aftermath of the 2020 presidential election, claims of widespread electoral fraud were widely circulated, particularly among supporters of the incumbent President Donald Trump.

Factionalism: Deep political polarization and partisanship, exacerbated by misinformation and inflammatory rhetoric, fueled tensions. Trump's encouragement of his supporters to "stop the steal" by marching to the Capitol amplified these divisions.

Riot: On January 6, 2021, a large crowd of President Trump's supporters stormed the U.S. Capitol in Washington, DC, aiming to disrupt the certification of the Electoral College results. The rioters breached security, causing significant damage, violence, and numerous injuries and some deaths. The incident led to numerous arrests and widespread condemnation, highlighting the dangers of factionalism, misinformation and, to be honest, a deplorable lack of civics instruction in the nation's primary schools.

THESIS 21

The spirit of encroachment [that] tends to consolidate the powers of all departments in one, and thus creating a real despotism.

The U.S. federal government has, at various times, consolidated power into bureaucratic departments in response to crises, perceived threats, and public fears. This process often centralizes authority and expands executive control, sometimes at the expense of civil liberties. Here are several examples:

THE ALIEN AND SEDITION ACTS (1798)

Context: During the Quasi-War with France, the Federalist-controlled government feared French influence and internal dissent.

Consolidation of Power: The Alien and Sedition Acts allowed the federal government to detain and deport non-citizens deemed dangerous and to criminalize speech critical of the government. These acts significantly expanded executive authority and curtailed freedoms, consolidating power in response to fears of foreign subversion.

THE ESPIONAGE AND SEDITION ACTS (1917–1918)

Context: During World War I, fears of espionage and internal subversion were heightened.

Consolidation of Power: These laws granted the federal government broad powers to suppress dissent, censor the press, and prosecute individuals for anti-war activities and speech. The Acts centralized authority under the federal government, limiting civil liberties in the name of national security.

THE NEW DEAL (1930S)

Context: The Great Depression prompted a massive federal response to economic collapse.

Consolidation of Power: President Franklin D. Roosevelt's New Deal created numerous federal agencies and programs, such as the Social Security Administration, the Securities and Exchange Commission, and the National Labor Relations Board. These entities centralized economic and social control, significantly expanding federal oversight and regulatory power in reaction to economic fears.

THE INCARCERATION OF JAPANESE AMERICANS (1942)

Context: After the attack on Pearl Harbor in 1941, there was widespread fear and suspicion of Japanese Americans as potential spies or saboteurs.

Consolidation of Power: Executive Order 9066 authorized the forced relocation and incarceration of over 120,000 Japanese Americans into internment camps. The federal government centralized authority to detain a specific ethnic group without due process, significantly curtailing civil liberties in the name of national security.

THE NATIONAL SECURITY ACT (1947)

Context: In the early Cold War period, fears of communist infiltration and global conflict dominated U.S. policy.

Consolidation of Power: The Act restructured the U.S. military and intelligence services, creating the Department of Defense, the Central Intelligence Agency (CIA), and the National Security Council (NSC). This restructuring centralized military and intelligence functions under a unified federal command, enhancing executive control over national security matters.

THE PATRIOT ACT (2001)

Context: The terrorist attacks on September 11, 2001, led to widespread fear of further attacks and demands for increased security.

Consolidation of Power: The Patriot Act expanded the federal government's surveillance capabilities, allowing for greater monitoring of communications, financial transactions, and personal data. The Act increased the powers of federal law enforcement and intelligence agencies, consolidating authority at the expense of civil liberties and privacy.

THE DEPARTMENT OF HOMELAND SECURITY (2002)

Context: In the wake of the 9/11 attacks, there was a perceived need for a coordinated federal response to domestic threats.

Consolidation of Power: The creation of the Department of Homeland Security (DHS) merged 22 federal agencies into a single department, centralizing authority over immigration, border security, disaster response, and counterterrorism. This reorganization consolidated significant power within the executive branch with the intention to enhance national security.

THE WAR ON DRUGS (1980S–PRESENT)

Context: Rising drug use and related violence led to public demand for a strong federal response.

Consolidation of Power: The federal government expanded its authority through policies and agencies focused on drug enforcement, such as the creation of the Drug Enforcement Administration (DEA). This war on drugs centralized law enforcement efforts and led to increased federal intervention in local and state matters, often resulting in the militarization of police forces and the erosion of civil liberties.

Washington's warning underscores the dangers of unchecked government authority that can be empowered by the violence and unrest mentioned in Thesis 20. When branches of government exceed their original constitutional bounds, it can threaten the original constitutional balance of power and the seeds of despotism begin to germinate.

Part II

HOW DO WE REPAIR THE DAMAGE DONE BY MODERN PARTISANSHIP?

Start by doing what's necessary; then do what's possible;
and suddenly you are doing the impossible.

—FRANCIS OF ASSISI

THESIS 22

*A candidate for political office can only accept campaign funds from
individual citizens qualified to vote for them.*

In the realm of political governance, the integrity of the electoral process stands as the cornerstone of democracy. It is imperative that those seeking public office remain beholden to the interests of their constituents, rather than being swayed by the influence of special interest groups or corporate entities. This principle is underscored by the historical precedent that has shaped our understanding of democratic governance.

Throughout history, we have witnessed the pernicious effects of undue influence on political candidates. From the days of ancient civilizations to the modern era, instances abound where the allegiance of elected officials has been compromised by the allure of financial support from powerful entities. Such influence undermines the fundamental tenets of democracy, eroding public trust and subverting the will of the people.

POST–CIVIL WAR TO THE EARLY 20TH CENTURY

The Civil War's aftermath saw political parties increasingly dependent on wealthy individuals like Jay Cooke, the Vanderbilts, and the Astors for financial support, a trend exacerbated by the lack of a civil service system. The first federal campaign finance law emerged in 1867, aimed at Navy yard workers, but it was the Pendleton Civil Service Reform Act of 1883 that broadened these restrictions to all federal civil service workers, pushing parties toward corporate and individual wealth for funding.

The election of 1896, with Mark Hanna's systematic fundraising from the business community for William McKinley, set a precedent for modern campaign financing, including commercial advertising. Following McKinley's assassination, Theodore Roosevelt's presidency initially fought against corporate influence but ultimately turned to wealthy backers for support, leading to calls for reform and the proposal for public financing and disclosure of campaign expenditures.

20TH-CENTURY REFORMS AND CHALLENGES

The Tillman Act of 1907 marked the first significant federal effort to restrict corporate contributions to political campaigns, albeit with limited enforcement. The Federal Election Campaign Act (FECA) of 1971 and its amendments in 1974, in response to the Watergate scandal, established a more robust framework for campaign finance regulation, including the creation of the Federal Election Commission. However, the Supreme Court's decision in *Buckley v. Valeo* (1976) struck down spending limits as unconstitutional, complicating reform efforts.

Despite various legislative attempts in the 1980s and 1990s to address campaign finance issues, significant reform was elusive until the Bipartisan Campaign Reform Act (BCRA) of 2002, also known as McCain-Feingold. This legislation sought to eliminate soft money contributions and regulate electioneering communications but faced constitutional challenges, including the landmark *Citizens United v. Federal Election Commission* decision in 2010, which significantly altered the landscape of campaign finance by allowing unlimited independent expenditures by corporations and unions.

MODERN IMPLICATIONS AND CONTINUING DEBATES

In the landmark case of *Citizens United v. Federal Election Commission* in January 2010, the U.S. Supreme Court ruled that the First Amendment prohibits the government from restricting independent political expenditures by corporations and unions. The Court's decision was grounded in the belief that free speech rights apply not only to individual citizens but also to associations of citizens, including corporations. This ruling overturned previous decisions that allowed for the prohibition of corporate spending on election-related communications, affirming that the First Amendment does not permit the government to limit political speech based on the speaker's identity. As a result, corporations and unions can now spend unlimited amounts on advocating for the election or defeat of candidates, though direct contributions to candidates or political parties remain prohibited. The evolution of campaign finance in the United States from the Jacksonian era to the present day reflects a complex interplay between democracy, corporate power, and regulatory efforts. Each phase of reform has sought to balance the need for political expression with concerns over undue influence, leading to a continuously shifting legal and political landscape. The ongoing debate over the role of money in politics remains a pivotal issue, with the Supreme Court's decisions playing a crucial role in shaping the boundaries of campaign finance law.

To safeguard the integrity of the electoral process given the modern

Supreme Court that views the constitution through a textualist lens, it is essential to separate money from speech and restrict campaign contributions to individual citizens who are qualified to vote for the candidate through a constitutional amendment. This action will uphold the sanctity of democratic representation and ensure that elected officials remain accountable to the electorate rather than beholden to special interests.

1. Prevent wealthy donors and corporate entities that are "outside the arena" from wielding disproportionate influence over the localized electoral process and government. This will promote fairness in political participation and make our political leadership less susceptible to the pressures exerted by outside donors seeking to advance their own agendas. This will foster a democracy where every voice carries equal weight and every citizen has an equal opportunity to engage in the political process, which will bolster public confidence in the integrity of the political system while enhancing the legitimacy of elected representatives.

THESIS 23

A candidate for political office should be limited to how many years they can serve to ensure the public benefit is not compromised by the power accumulated for their self-benefit.

Throughout the annals of history, civilizations have grappled with the challenge of balancing stability with the need for periodic renewal in leadership. Ancient Athens provides a compelling example, where the rotation of officials through strict term limits was instrumental in fostering a vibrant democratic ethos. By preventing the entrenchment of power and promoting the active participation of citizens, term limits played a pivotal role in maintaining the vitality of Athenian democracy.

In the early history of the United States, George Washington set a critical precedent by voluntarily limiting his time in office, underscoring the importance of avoiding the concentration of power. Washington's decision to step down after two terms was a powerful statement that the presidency should not become a position of indefinite rule. This concept of limiting executive power was not initially extended to representatives in Congress, who were seen as less susceptible to the same risks due to their collective nature and frequent elections.

However, in the modern political environment of the U.S., the dynamics have shifted significantly. Today, representatives wield much more power and are able to utilize the resources of their positions to gain an elevated advantage over challengers. This entrenched incumbency, combined with hyper-partisanship and a growing disconnect between public desires and legislative action, has led to widespread disillusionment with Congress. Congressional approval ratings remain consistently low, while the reelection rate for incumbents is remarkably high, suggesting a need for reform.

The concept of term limits has garnered significant attention as a possible solution to these issues. Proponents argue that term limits could introduce fresh perspectives, curtail the dominance of career politicians, and mitigate the influence of big donors and special interests that currently dominate the political landscape. By rotating representatives and ensuring that no individual holds office for too long, term limits could foster a more dynamic and responsive legislative body, better aligned with the needs and desires of the American people.

THE DRAWBACKS OF CAREER POLITICIANS

Career politicians, those who have turned their service in Congress into a long-term profession, present a significant challenge to legislative efficacy and responsiveness. The increasing tenure of members of Congress contrasts sharply with the broader American workforce's median tenure of just over four years. This disparity underscores the problem: congressional members often prioritize reelection efforts and donor interests over public service and legislative problem-solving.

FINANCIAL IMPERATIVES IN CONGRESSIONAL CAMPAIGNS

Campaign financing plays a pivotal role in congressional elections, with the top spenders winning a significant majority of races. The reliance on campaign contributions from big donors and special interests not only diverts time and resources from legislative duties but also skews priorities toward those with the means to influence election outcomes rather than the general public's welfare.

INCENTIVES FOR PARTISANSHIP AND SHORT-TERM FOCUS

The current structure fosters a political environment where partisanship and short-term thinking prevail. The necessity to secure reelection and the influence of special interests create incentives for members of Congress to focus on immediate gains, partisan bickering, and blame-shifting rather than addressing long-term national issues and engaging in bipartisan cooperation.

THE PROMISE OF TERM LIMITS

Term limits could fundamentally alter the incentive structure in Washington by removing the perpetual cycle of reelection, thereby cutting the ties to big donors and special interests. Without the pressure of securing future campaigns, politicians might prioritize genuine public service, encouraging bipartisan collaboration and a focus on long-term solutions over short-term electoral gains. Term limits could usher in a new era of governance, marked by a diversity of experience, fresh ideas, and a return to civility, as members of Congress view their roles as temporary public service rather than lifelong careers.

Ultimately, term limits offer a pathway to revitalizing American democracy by ensuring that power truly resides with the people, through representatives who are more focused on serving their country than preserving their political careers.

The imperative of imposing term limits on political officeholders resonates deeply with the foundational principles of democracy and governance. History serves as a poignant reminder of the perils associated with unchecked tenure in office, where power accumulation can lead to complacency, corruption, and the erosion of public trust. Therefore, the institution of term limits emerges as a vital mechanism to safeguard against these threats and uphold the integrity of democratic governance.

THESIS 24

The source of income received by political candidates or office holders must be fully disclosed.

The imperative of ensuring full disclosure of income by political candidates and officeholders cannot be overstated, as it lies at the heart of maintaining the integrity and accountability of democratic governance. Throughout history, clandestine financial dealings and undisclosed sources of income have been synonymous with corruption, eroding public trust and undermining the legitimacy of political systems. Therefore, implementing stringent disclosure requirements is not just desirable but essential in upholding the principles of transparency and ethical conduct in politics.

Drawing upon historical examples, such as the enactment of the Lex Julia during the reign of Julius Caesar in ancient Rome, underscores the enduring importance of transparency in financial matters. This legislation, which mandated public officials to disclose their financial assets and income sources, serves as a testament to the recognition of transparency as a cornerstone of responsible governance. By learning from these historical lessons, modern democracies can appreciate the critical role of income disclosure in fostering public trust and preventing abuses of power.

In contemporary contexts, scandals like the Panama Papers have laid bare the consequences of financial secrecy in politics, exposing the potential for corruption and unethical behavior when financial dealings remain concealed. By contrast, comprehensive income disclosure requirements serve as a bulwark against such abuses, providing citizens with vital information to hold their elected representatives accountable. When voters are empowered with knowledge about the financial interests of their leaders, they can make informed decisions and demand greater transparency and accountability in government.

Moreover, income disclosure acts as a vital tool for preventing conflicts of interest and ensuring that elected officials prioritize the public interest over personal gain. By shedding light on potential financial entanglements, disclosure requirements help mitigate the risk of corruption and unethical behavior among political leaders. This transparency not only strengthens public trust in government but also reinforces the democratic principle that elected officials are accountable to the people they serve.

THESIS 25

Elected members of Congress must not partake in a retirement plan.
They should receive Social Security like the rest of us.

Ensuring that elected members of Congress are not enrolled in a separate retirement plan but rather rely on Social Security, like the rest of the citizenry, is a crucial step toward promoting fairness, accountability, and empathy in governance. Throughout history, examples abound of political leaders who prioritized the interests of the people they served over personal privileges, thereby setting a precedent for selfless leadership and public service.

Consider the case of Cincinnatus, the revered Roman statesman and farmer who relinquished absolute power after just 15 days to return to his humble life. By voluntarily surrendering authority and eschewing the trappings of wealth and privilege, Cincinnatus epitomized the ideal of a citizen-leader committed to the welfare of the republic. His example serves as a timeless reminder that elected officials should prioritize the common good above personal enrichment.

In modern times, the spirit of selfless leadership is exemplified by figures like President Harry Truman, who, upon leaving office, chose to decline lucrative offers and instead lived modestly on his pension. Truman's decision reflected a deep-seated belief in the principles of equality and humility, demonstrating that elected officials should lead by example in matters of financial stewardship and ethical conduct.

Furthermore, the exclusion of elected members of Congress from a separate retirement plan aligns with the fundamental principles of democratic governance. In a system where representatives are meant to serve the interests of the people, it is essential to avoid creating a class of political elites insulated from the financial challenges faced by ordinary citizens. By relying on Social Security like their constituents, elected officials are more likely to remain attuned to the needs and concerns of the broader population.

Moreover, the absence of a separate retirement plan for members of Congress serves as a safeguard against conflicts of interest and undue influence. When politicians are not beholden to special interests or corporate donors for their retirement-security, they are better positioned to make decisions based solely on the merits of the issues at hand. This fosters a more transparent and accountable political system, where elected officials can prioritize the public interest without fear of reprisal or undue influence.

THESIS 26

End the practice of dividing the congressional chambers along party lines and have all state delegations sitting together in both legislative houses.

Ending the practice of dividing the congressional chambers along party lines and instead having all state delegations sit together in both legislative houses is a crucial step toward fostering unity, bipartisanship, and effective governance. Throughout history, examples abound of the detrimental effects of partisan division on legislative productivity and national cohesion, underscoring the need for a more inclusive and collaborative approach to lawmaking.

Consider the case of the early United States Congress, where political factions were often deeply entrenched and bitterly divided along ideological lines. This partisan gridlock frequently hampered legislative progress and hindered efforts to address pressing national issues. The bitter debates over issues such as slavery and tariffs culminated in sectionalism and, ultimately, civil war, highlighting the dangers of unchecked partisan animosity.

Similarly, in more recent times, the hyper-partisan atmosphere in Congress has led to legislative paralysis, government shutdowns, and a growing sense of disillusionment among the American people. The practice of seating members along party lines has only served to exacerbate this polarization, fostering an "us versus them" mentality that undermines cooperation and compromise.

In contrast, seating members of Congress by state delegation promotes a spirit of cooperation and encourages lawmakers to prioritize the common interests of their home state over nationalized partisan politics. By fostering relationships across party lines, we create an environment that helps facilitate dialogue, consensus-building, and the pursuit of pragmatic solutions to complex challenges.

Moreover, seating members of Congress by state delegation reflects the principles of federalism and representative democracy upon which the United States was founded. It ensures that each state's interests are adequately represented and empowers local lawmakers to work collaboratively.

THESIS 27

If the Senate maintains a filibuster rule, then the actual filibuster must take place and must adhere to the subject of legislation under debate.

The filibuster, initially designed to safeguard minority interests and encourage robust debate, has undergone a significant transformation over time. Originally, filibusters required senators to engage in lengthy speeches to stall or block legislation, serving as a tangible expression of dissent and a mechanism for negotiation and compromise.

However, in the past 50 years, the filibuster has been increasingly abused as a procedural tactic, detached from its original purpose. Senators now merely signal their intent to filibuster, bringing legislative proceedings to a halt without engaging in substantive debate. This misuse undermines the democratic process, allowing minority factions to wield disproportionate power without constructive engagement.

To address this issue, it is crucial to amend the filibuster rule to mandate genuine filibusters that relate directly to the legislation under consideration. Requiring senators to actively debate on the Senate floor reinstates accountability and encourages meaningful dialogue and negotiation. By restoring this accountability mechanism, the filibuster can once again serve as a check on majority power while fostering compromise and consensus-building.

This proposed reform aligns with historical precedent, echoing an era when senators engaged in principled debates to advance their positions. By reintroducing this requirement, the Senate can restore public confidence in its ability to govern effectively and uphold democratic norms.

THESIS 28

End the practice of omnibus bills: any bill must pertain to one subject only, and that subject should be in the title.

The proliferation of omnibus bills, encompassing multiple disparate provisions within a single legislative package, undermines the fundamental principles of transparency and accountability in the legislative process. This practice often leads to opaque decision-making, as lawmakers may be compelled to support or oppose entire bills based on individual provisions unrelated to the bill's primary purpose.

To illustrate the significance of this issue, one can look back to the founding principles of legislative governance. The framers of the Constitution envisioned a deliberative process where each piece of legislation was scrutinized on its own merits, ensuring that lawmakers and the public could fully understand and assess the implications of proposed laws. However, the advent of omnibus bills has deviated from this intent, allowing for the inclusion of unrelated provisions that may bypass thorough scrutiny and debate.

Furthermore, the use of omnibus bills has historically been associated with instances of legislative overreach and political maneuvering. By bundling unrelated measures into a single bill, lawmakers may seek to obscure controversial provisions or circumvent opposition, thus undermining the democratic process and eroding public trust in government institutions. The first major omnibus bill enacted in the United States was the Compromise of 1850, which had five disparate provisions designed by Senator Henry Clay of Kentucky. His purpose was to pacify sectional differences that threatened to provoke the secession of the slave states. The Fugitive Slave Act was the most infamous of the five compromise components, and was almost universally excoriated by abolitionists, the chief exception being Senator Daniel Webster of Massachusetts, who prioritized preservation of the Union. Senator Thomas

Hart Benton, a Missouri slaveholder, opposed the omnibus compromise as an "unmanageable mass of incongruous bills, each an impediment to the other."

While this bill did not pass as the official Compromise of 1850, it got the ball rolling. To satisfy members of Congress, Stephen A. Douglas separated the Compromise back into five separate bills and got it passed. Ultimately, disunion and civil war were delayed for a decade. Interestingly, it was the 1861 Constitution of the Confederate States that first attempted to ban omnibus legislation, requiring that every bill "shall relate to but one subject, and that shall be expressed in the title."

Since the Congressional Budget Act of 1974, omnibus budget bills have become the norm, streamlining multiple appropriations into one package. However, this approach poses risks to legislative clarity and financial prudence. Congress has only managed to pass its appropriations on schedule four times since then, often delaying even the preliminary budget blueprint. The comprehensive size of omnibus bills leaves little time for detailed examination, allowing for the inclusion of unrelated or contentious policy riders. The necessity to approve the bill in its entirety also forces legislators to endorse items they may not support, to avoid being blamed for potential government shutdowns. Such practices compromise the democratic process, restricting debate and the chance for amendments, and facilitate fiscal recklessness by concealing spending increases and pet projects, diminishing public oversight and accountability. This corrupted process makes it almost impossible to reign in the budget deficit as legislatures are incentivized to include funding for their personal pet projects.

THESIS 29

*The Electoral College should not be party appointees nor
winner-take-all.*

The Electoral College, as it stands today, has been a cornerstone of American presidential elections since the founding of the nation. However, its partisan nature and the winner-take-all system employed by most states have led to various criticisms and calls for reform. Transitioning to a nonpartisan and proportional system could address many of these concerns, fostering a more equitable and democratic electoral process. Importantly, the Electoral College remains vital for electing a president of a federalized republic where the states are voting members, but it must be reformed to better serve its purpose.

MITIGATING PARTISAN BIAS

A primary critique of the current Electoral College is its susceptibility to partisan manipulation. In most states, the winning party secures all the electoral votes, which can disproportionately amplify their victory. This system often marginalizes voters from the minority party within a state, effectively silencing their electoral voice. A nonpartisan approach to the Electoral College, where electors are chosen based on their qualifications and commitment to represent the electorate rather than party allegiance, could help mitigate this bias. By focusing on the integrity and impartiality of electors, the electoral process would better reflect the true will of the people, rather than the strategic interests of political parties.

ENHANCING FAIR REPRESENTATION

The winner-take-all system creates significant disparities in representation. Candidates tend to focus their campaigns on a few battleground states, neglecting the majority of the country where the outcome is more predictable. This leads to an uneven distribution of campaign resources and political attention, undermining the principle of equal representation. A proportional allocation of electoral votes, where each candidate receives votes corresponding to their share of the popular vote in each state, would ensure that every vote matters. This system would compel candidates to engage with a broader spectrum of voters, fostering a more inclusive and representative electoral process.

REDUCING ELECTORAL DISPARITIES

The current Electoral College system can result in a president elected without winning the popular vote, as seen in several recent elections. This discrepancy between the popular vote and the Electoral College outcome undermines public confidence in the democratic process. A proportional system would reduce the likelihood of such disparities by aligning electoral votes more closely with the national popular vote. This alignment would enhance the legitimacy of the election outcome and reinforce the democratic principle that the presidency should reflect the choice of the majority of Americans.

ENCOURAGING POLITICAL MODERATION

A nonpartisan and proportional Electoral College could also encourage political moderation. The winner-take-all system incentivizes candidates to adopt extreme positions to secure their base in swing states, often leading to polarization. In contrast, a proportional system would reward candidates who appeal to a broader electorate, promoting more moderate and consensus-driven policies. This shift could help bridge the partisan divide and foster a more cooperative political environment.

PROMOTING NATIONAL UNITY

Finally, a nonpartisan and proportional Electoral College would promote national unity. The current system often exacerbates regional divisions, as the focus on swing states can make voters in solidly red or blue states feel neglected. By ensuring that every vote contributes to the overall electoral outcome, a proportional system would encourage candidates to address the concerns of all Americans, regardless of their state's political leaning. This inclusivity would strengthen the sense of national unity and shared purpose.

Preserving the Role of States in a Federalized Republic

Despite its flaws, the Electoral College is still vital for electing a president in a federalized republic where the states are voting members. The founders designed the Electoral College to balance the influence of populous and less populous states, ensuring that all states have a meaningful role in the election process. This system acknowledges the federal structure of the United States, where both the national and state governments share sovereignty. By maintaining the Electoral College, we preserve the principle that the presidency should be decided not just by a direct national popular vote but through the collective will of the states as distinct entities.

Reforming Without Abandoning

Reforming the Electoral College to make it nonpartisan and proportional does not mean abandoning the institution. Instead, it means refining it to better fulfill its intended purpose in a modern context. By addressing partisan biases and the winner-take-all system, we can enhance the Electoral College's ability to fairly and accurately reflect the electorate's will while preserving its foundational role in our federalized republic.

In conclusion, transitioning to a nonpartisan and proportional Electoral College would address many of the shortcomings of the current system. It would mitigate partisan bias, enhance fair representation, reduce electoral disparities, encourage political moderation, and promote national unity. Importantly, it would do so while preserving the essential role of the states in our federal system, ensuring that the Electoral College continues to serve as a cornerstone of American democracy.

THESIS 30

The Senate and the House must return to their original role of checks and balances with each other.

THESIS 31

For the Senate and House to check each other, the legislative branches must have different constituencies.

THESIS 32

Repeal the 17ᵗʰ Amendment so the Senate can return to its original constitutional role as representing state governments.

The framers of the Constitution designed the Senate and the House to serve different purposes. The House, with its frequent elections and smaller districts, was meant to be directly responsive to the people. The Senate, with its longer terms and original election by state legislatures, was intended to represent state governments and provide a stabilizing influence.

The Great Compromise of 1787 was a pivotal moment in American history that established the framework for the bicameral legislature. This compromise resolved a deadlock between larger states, which favored representation based on population (the Virginia Plan), and smaller states, which favored equal representation (the New Jersey Plan). By creating the House of Representatives, with representation based on population, and the Senate, with equal representation for each state, the framers ensured that both populous and less populous states had a balanced influence on federal legislation. This structure allowed the Senate to act as a check on the more directly responsive House, fostering balanced and deliberate lawmaking.

Today, both the Senate and the House are elected by popular vote, leading to increased partisan polarization. Senators, who once acted as representatives of state interests, now often prioritize nationalized party agendas over state-specific concerns. This shift has contributed to legislative gridlock and politicization of processes, such as the confirmation of Supreme Court nominees.

The 17th Amendment, ratified in 1913, changed the election of senators from state legislatures to direct popular vote. While this change aimed to reduce corruption and increase democratic participation, it fundamentally altered the Senate's role in representing state governments. Instead of removing the state's role in selecting senators, the amendment should have clarified how each state was to select its respective senator so there is a uniform method of selection that is responsible and accountable to the respective state constituencies. I personally feel the senator should be appointed by the governor and approved by the state legislature. If the state legislature fails to act within a certain period of time, then the appointment stands.

Before the 17th Amendment, senators were accountable to state legislatures, ensuring that state interests were directly represented at the federal level. For instance, during the debate over the Tariff of 1828, known as the "Tariff of Abominations," senators advocated for state economic interests, balancing the demands of industrial and agricultural states. This balance helped maintain the Union's economic stability and highlighted the Senate's role in protecting state sovereignty within the federal system.

The direct election of senators has shifted their focus from state-specific issues to national political trends and party loyalty. This shift has diminished the Senate's effectiveness in checking federal overreach and maintaining a balance of power between the states and the federal government. The politicization of the Senate's advice and consent role in judicial nominations reflects this broader trend. Senators now prioritize partisan considerations over nuanced deliberation and state interests, contributing to a more polarized and less functional legislative process.

By reestablishing distinct roles for the House and Senate and ensuring that the Senate represents state interests, Congress can better fulfill its constitutional responsibilities. This approach would lead to reduced political gridlock and a stronger representation of the diverse interests that make up the United States.

THESIS 33

The districts of members of the House of Representatives should be reduced in size to reflect a closer connectivity with the people of the district.

In the early years of the United States, the House of Representatives was designed to be the branch of Congress closest to the people. The original ratio of representatives to constituents was approximately 1:30,000, allowing representatives to maintain close connections with their constituents. This proximity fostered a strong sense of accountability and responsiveness.

Over time, as the population of the United States has grown, the size of House districts has increased significantly. The Permanent Apportionment Act of 1929 capped the number of representatives at 435, leading to larger districts as the population grew. Today, each member of the House represents an average of approximately 760,000 people, a far cry from the original ratio.

The large size of contemporary districts has several negative consequences. Representatives find it increasingly difficult to maintain direct contact with their constituents, and the sheer number of people they represent makes it challenging to address individual and community-specific concerns. This disconnect can lead to a sense of disenfranchisement among voters, a perception that their representatives are out of touch with local issues, and a lack of trust in the political process.

Reducing the size of representative districts can also help mitigate the issue of gerrymandering by increasing the number of districts, thereby making it more challenging to draw boundaries that systematically favor one party.

With smaller districts, the demographic diversity within each district tends to be less pronounced, reducing the ability to manipulate boundaries to create safe seats for a particular party. This leads to more competitive elections and representatives who are more accountable to their constituents, as the impact of gerrymandering diminishes with the increased difficulty of strategically designing numerous small districts to achieve a particular political outcome.

The United States is in the top ten countries with the highest percentage of constituents per single representative. This list includes Indonesia, Brazil, Bangladesh, Nigeria, Pakistan, Afghanistan, European Union, India, and China—not normally the type of "democracies" we like to be compared to. To pour salt in the wound, we are the third highest in the world. Our closest European allies that have the most populated democracies (England, France, and Germany) have between 95,000 to 115,000 persons per representative.

The previous point leads us to the common concern that increasing the number of representatives would lead to a less functional House of Representatives. However, this is not necessarily the case.

A larger House could enhance deliberation and representation by bringing in a more diverse array of voices and perspectives. Historical examples from other countries with larger legislative bodies, such as the United Kingdom's House of Commons, (650) and Germany's Bundestag (735 in 2024), demonstrate that larger legislatures can function effectively and efficiently.

Advances in technology and modern communication methods can facilitate the functioning of a larger House. Digital platforms and tools can streamline legislative processes, improve communication among representatives, and enhance transparency and accessibility. These tools can help manage the increased number of representatives and ensure that the legislative body operates smoothly.

Increasing the number of representatives could also help mitigate extreme partisanship, especially if incorporating the other policy initiatives in this chapter. With more representatives in the context of the other reforms, the influence of any single party or faction is diluted, leading to more coalition-building and compromise. This environment can foster a more collaborative and less polarized legislative process.

Reducing the size of House districts and increasing the number of representatives is a crucial step toward enhancing the connection between representatives and their constituents and ensuring effective governance. A larger House of Representatives would not necessarily lead to dysfunction; instead, it would enhance representation, facilitate more comprehensive deliberation, and mitigate partisanship.

THESIS 34

No elected official can leave elected office and work in any "position of influence" (Board of Trustees or be employed as a lobbyist) with a 501c4 for a period equal to his/her time in office.

The wisdom of Thesis 34 is self-evident in its potential to reduce corruption and conflicts of interest within the political class. Here are some examples of how the revolving door between elected office and influential positions has corrupted politics

1. **Conflicts of Interest:**

    *   **Example:** Former Congressman Billy Tauzin, who played a key role in passing the Medicare Modernization Act of 2003, left Congress to become the head of the Pharmaceutical Research and Manufacturers of America (PhRMA). This act was highly beneficial to the pharmaceutical industry, raising concerns about whether his legislative actions were influenced by future job prospects.

    *   **Impact:** Such moves can create conflicts of interest, where officials may make decisions that benefit their future employers rather than the public.

2. **Undue Influence and Access:**

    - **Example:** After leaving office, former Senator Chris Dodd became the chairman and CEO of the Motion Picture Association of America (MPAA). His transition exemplifies how former lawmakers leverage their connections and knowledge to influence policy in favor of specific industries.

    - **Impact:** This revolving door can lead to former officials having undue influence on current lawmakers, effectively allowing special interests to shape legislation and policy.

3. **Erosion of Public Trust:**

    - **Example:** Former House Majority Leader Eric Cantor lost his reelection bid and shortly thereafter took a high-paying job with a Wall Street investment bank. His swift move to the private sector raised questions about whether his legislative actions were influenced by potential job opportunities.

    - **Impact:** Such career transitions can erode public trust in elected officials, as constituents may believe that their representatives are more interested in lucrative post-office careers than in serving the public good.

4. **Policy Decisions Favoring Special Interests:**

    - **Example:** Former Secretary of Defense Dick Cheney, who served as CEO of Halliburton before his tenure in government, was criticized for the company's significant contracts during the Iraq War, which some argued benefited from Cheney's former connections. Support work to U.S. military operations and U.S.-funded reconstruction projects made up $2.1 billion of the company's $5.5 billion of revenue in the first quarter of 2004.

    - The contracts also contributed $32 million of operating profit to Halliburton, which was run from 1995 to 2000 by

Vice President Dick Cheney.

- **Impact:** The perception (or reality) that policy decisions are made to benefit former or future employers rather than the public can undermine the integrity of government actions.

5. **Legislative Capture:**

- **Example:** Many former legislators become lobbyists, such as former Senator Trent Lott, who became a lobbyist for various industries after leaving office. This can lead to legislative capture, where the interests of a few outweigh the needs of the many.

- **Impact:** Legislative capture can result in policies that disproportionately favor wealthy corporations and special interest groups, rather than the broader population.

By implementing a cooling-off period equal to the time served in office before allowing former officials to take positions of influence, this thesis helps mitigate these issues. This would:

- **Reduce Conflicts of Interest:** Officials would be less likely to make decisions based on future job prospects.
- **Decrease Undue Influence:** It would limit the ability of former officials to immediately leverage their connections for private gain.
- **Restore Public Trust:** Constituents might have more confidence in the integrity of their representatives.
- **Promote Fair Policy Making:** Policies would more likely reflect the public interest rather than the interests of specific industries or organizations.
- **Prevent Legislative Capture:** It would help ensure that legislative processes remain more balanced and less dominated by special interests.

It's time this deplorable process is ended.

THESIS 35

*Citizens of the Republic should be governed
more by the government closest to them.*

THESIS 36

*The state government is the closest government to the people due to its
comprehensive constitutional authority, legislative power, regulatory
oversight, and direct accountability to residents through elections
and governance.*

The principle that citizens of the Republic should be governed more by the government closest to them—namely, their state government—is rooted in the ideals of federalism and the belief in localized decision-making. This notion underscores the importance of accountability, responsiveness, and tailored governance to meet the unique needs of diverse communities. However, over the course of U.S. history, there has been a notable shift toward increased federal control over areas traditionally managed by states, such as education, health care, and infrastructure. This shift has introduced several challenges and potential detriments to the political and social fabric of the nation. Given the vast local complexity and diversity of the United States, state-level governance is not just preferable but necessary to effectively govern such a large nation through democratic methods.

LOCAL ACCOUNTABILITY AND RESPONSIVENESS

State governments are inherently more accessible and accountable to their residents compared to the distant federal government. Local officials are often members of the community, directly experiencing the issues they govern. This proximity fosters a sense of responsibility and responsiveness. For instance, state governments can quickly address local crises, such as natural disasters, with tailored responses that reflect the immediate needs of their citizens. This direct line of accountability ensures that elected officials are more attuned to their constituents' concerns and can be swiftly held accountable through local elections and civic engagement.

POLICIES TAILORED TO LOCAL NEEDS

The United States is a vast nation with a remarkable diversity of cultures, economies, and social norms. States possess the unique ability to craft policies that reflect their specific cultural, economic, and social contexts. For example, agricultural states can prioritize farming subsidies and regulations beneficial to their local economies, while urban states might focus on public transportation and infrastructure. This flexibility allows for more effective and relevant policymaking. A one-size-fits-all approach, often necessitated by federal governance, can overlook the distinct characteristics and needs of different states, leading to inefficiencies and dissatisfaction among residents.

ENCOURAGEMENT OF INNOVATION AND EXPERIMENTATION

The concept of states serving as "laboratories of democracy" is a cornerstone of American federalism, but the notion has been corrupted into the idea that states can experiment with novel policies and programs on a smaller scale as "preparation" for nationwide adoption. Massachusetts' health care reform in 2006, which later served as a model for the Affordable Care Act, exemplifies this principle. Such experimentation fosters innovation and allows for a diversity of approaches to solving problems, which should be studied and emulated by other states if successful, but which should not serve as an excuse for the federal government to take one state's solution and impose it on the remaining 49.

EXPANSION OF FEDERAL POWER IN STATE RESPONSIBILITIES

The U.S. has experienced significant shifts toward federal control over areas traditionally managed by states, often in response to national crises or perceived inefficiencies in state governance.

Education: The No Child Left Behind Act (NCLB) of 2001 expanded federal involvement in education, imposing standardized testing requirements and accountability measures on states. While aimed at improving educational outcomes, NCLB often disregarded local educational priorities and needs.

Health Care: The Affordable Care Act (ACA) of 2010 significantly increased federal oversight of health insurance markets and Medicaid. While the ACA aimed to expand health care coverage, it also imposed federal standards that sometimes clashed with state-specific health needs and priorities.

Infrastructure: Federal transportation funding and regulations have increasingly dictated state infrastructure projects and often come with stipulations that may not align with local needs or preferences.

The expansion of federal power often results in the imposition of federal mandates that disregard local priorities and needs. For instance, the No Child Left Behind Act imposed standardized testing requirements on all states, without consideration for the unique educational challenges and priorities of each state. This loss of local autonomy can lead to policies that are ineffective or even harmful in certain contexts.

The expansion of federal agencies and regulations creates a more complex and cumbersome governmental structure. This increased bureaucracy can result in slower responses to local issues and an overall decrease in governmental efficiency. State and local governments, which are closer to the issues, are often better positioned to act.

When policies are made at the federal level, it becomes harder for citizens to hold specific lawmakers accountable for decisions that affect their daily lives. This dilution of accountability can lead to voter apathy and a sense of disconnection from the political process. In contrast, state and local governments provide more direct channels for citizens to influence policy and hold their representatives accountable.

Federal regulations often result in one-size-fits-all policies that do not account for the diverse ecological and economic conditions across different states. For example, environmental regulations that are suitable for one region may be overly restrictive or insufficiently protective in another. This lack of flexibility can lead to suboptimal outcomes and increased tensions between state and federal authorities.

The historical shift toward greater federal control in the U.S., while sometimes necessary, has led to a loss of local autonomy, increased bureaucracy, diluted accountability, and one-size-fits-all policies that may not serve the best interests of diverse communities. Given the vast local complexity and diversity of the United States, state-level governance is essential to effectively manage such a large nation through democratic methods. By emphasizing state-level governance, the U.S. can return to a more balanced federalist system that respects the unique needs and preferences of its varied populace, ensuring a more effective and representative democracy.

THESIS 37

Services to the citizenry's well-being should be the primary responsibility of the State.

The notion that services to the citizenry's well-being should be the primary responsibility of the state is deeply rooted in the traditions of the American federal system. This principle emphasizes the importance of localized governance in addressing the diverse needs of communities across the United States. Over the past half-century, however, there has been a significant shift toward increased federal control over areas traditionally managed by state governments, such as primary education, local health care, mental health services, and welfare. This shift has led to various challenges and, arguably, a deterioration in the quality of these essential services.

HISTORICAL CONTEXT AND FEDERALISM

The United States was founded on the principles of federalism, where power is divided between national and state governments. This division was intended to allow states the flexibility to address their unique needs and priorities, fostering innovation and responsiveness. Historically, states have been responsible for services directly impacting the well-being of their citizens, including education, health care, mental health services, and welfare. This localized approach ensured that policies and programs could be tailored to the specific cultural, economic, and social contexts of each state.

PRIMARY EDUCATION

Deterioration Due to Federal Control

Over the past several decades, federal intervention in primary education has increased significantly. The No Child Left Behind Act (NCLB) of 2001 is a prime example. While well-intentioned, NCLB imposed standardized testing requirements and accountability measures on all states, regardless of their unique educational challenges and priorities. This one-size-fits-all approach often overlooked the distinct needs of local schools and communities.

Impact on Education Quality

The increased focus on standardized testing has led to a narrowing of the curriculum, with schools emphasizing test preparation over holistic education. This has resulted in reduced emphasis on subjects like history and civics, which are crucial for an informed citizenry, as well as art, music, and physical education, which are important for the overall development of students.

Benefits of State Responsibility

When states are responsible for primary education, they can develop policies that reflect the specific needs of their students and communities. Their ability to tailor educational approaches to local needs has resulted in better outcomes for students.

LOCAL HEALTH CARE

Deterioration Due to Federal Control

The Affordable Care Act (ACA) of 2010 significantly increased federal oversight of health insurance markets and Medicaid. While the ACA aimed to expand health care coverage, it also imposed federal standards that sometimes clashed with state-specific health needs and priorities. States lost some of their autonomy in designing health care programs that best suited their populations.

Impact on Health Care Quality

Federal regulations often fail to account for the unique health care challenges faced by different states. For example, rural states with large, sparsely populated areas have different health care needs compared to densely populated urban states. The imposition of uniform federal standards can lead to inefficiencies and gaps in health care delivery, particularly in areas that already struggle with access to medical services.

Benefits of State Responsibility

States that retain control over their health care systems can develop innovative solutions tailored to their specific challenges. For example, Vermont's single-payer health care initiative and Oregon's Medicaid reform efforts demonstrate how state-level control can lead to effective and innovative health care solutions. These states can address unique local health issues more effectively than a distant federal bureaucracy.

MENTAL HEALTH SERVICES

Deterioration Due to Federal Control

Mental health services have also seen increased federal involvement, particularly through Medicaid and other federal programs. Federal funding is essential to maintain current access to Medicaid, but the strings attached to this funding can limit the flexibility of states to design and implement mental health programs that meet local needs.

Impact on Mental Health Services

The lack of flexibility often results in a mismatch between the services provided and the actual needs of the community. For instance, some states might require more resources for community-based mental health services, while others might need more inpatient facilities. Federal oversight can lead to a one-size-fits-all approach that fails to address these local variations effectively.

The Impact of Reagan Tax Cuts on Mental Health Services

The mental health services landscape in the United States experienced significant changes following the Reagan administration's tax cuts in the 1980s. Prior to this period, federal funding played a crucial role in supporting state-run mental health programs, which had become heavily dependent on this financial assistance over the preceding decades. The Community Mental Health Act of 1963, for example, had established a robust framework for federal support, leading to the creation of numerous community mental health centers across the country. These centers relied on continuous federal funding to provide essential services.

However, the Reagan administration's tax cuts, part of a broader agenda to appropriately reduce federal spending and shift responsibilities to the states, resulted in substantial budget reductions for various social programs, including mental health services. The federal government's support for these programs dwindled significantly, leaving states to fill the financial gap. Unfortunately, most states were not prepared to replace the lost federal revenue with their own funds, leading to a decline in the availability and quality of mental health services.

States, grappling with their own budget constraints, struggled to maintain the levels of care and support that had been established under federal funding. The reduction in resources led to the closure of many community mental health centers, reduced services, and a growing number of individuals with mental health issues not receiving the care they needed. This period marked a significant setback for mental health care in the United States, with many of the gains made in previous century being eroded due to the abrupt withdrawal of federal financial support. The long-term effects of these changes are still felt today, as the mental health system continues to face challenges in providing adequate care to all who need it.

In my own home state of South Carolina, the sprawling 160-acre campus of the Mental Health Facility, locally known as "Bull Street," with its hundreds of thousands of square feet of space, was turned into a political football between the governor and the department of mental health over which entity had the right to sell off all the property and benefit from the millions of dollars that would be derived on the liquidation of almost 180 years of investment. With that debate settled, the property has now been turned into a neighborhood of luxury apartments and retail stores anchored with a minor league ball field.

Not surprisingly, small businesses, residents, and shoppers in downtown Columbia are challenged by the large numbers of homeless with mental health issues scattered throughout the city with nowhere else to go and no family able to advocate for them.

CONCLUSION

The tradition of state responsibility in providing services for the citizenry's well-being is a cornerstone of the American federal system. Over the past half-century, the shift toward increased federal control over primary education, local health care, mental health services, and welfare has led to various challenges and a deterioration in the quality of these services. By reaffirming the primary responsibility of states in these areas, the United States can ensure more responsive, effective, and tailored solutions that better meet the diverse needs of its citizens. Re-emphasizing state control in these critical areas aligns with the foundational principles of federalism and can lead to a more effective and representative governance system.

THESIS 38

*Hearings by legislative committees should only be shared publicly
through transcripts and end video recording except for security purposes.*

Public hearings by legislative committees are a cornerstone of democratic governance, providing a platform for transparency, accountability, and thorough fact-finding. However, the modern practice of video recording these hearings has increasingly shifted the focus from genuine investigation to social media theatrics and political grandstanding. This essay argues for the necessity of requiring full attendance by committee members and limiting the dissemination of these hearings to transcripts, except for security purposes. This reform would enhance the integrity of legislative processes, reduce politicization, and ensure that hearings serve their intended purpose of uncovering the truth and crafting effective policies.

THE PROBLEM WITH CURRENT PRACTICES

Social Media and Fundraising Exploitation

The widespread availability of video recordings has transformed legislative hearings into opportunities for political performance rather than serious inquiry. Elected representatives often use these platforms to deliver sound bites tailored for social media, aiming to boost their visibility and fundraising efforts rather than engage in substantive discussions. This shift detracts from the original purpose of hearings, which is to gather facts, analyze information, and make informed decisions.

Partial Attendance by Legislators

A common issue in current legislative hearings is the tendency of representatives to attend only the portions relevant to their questioning. They arrive for their turn, deliver prepared remarks or questions, and then leave, missing the broader context and the insights shared by other participants. This behavior undermines the collaborative nature of the hearings and leads to fragmented understanding and less effective legislative outcomes.

Benefits of Requiring Full Attendance and Transcripts

Ensuring Comprehensive Engagement

Mandating full attendance by committee members would ensure that all legislators are present for the entirety of the hearings. This requirement would foster a more collaborative and comprehensive approach to fact-finding, as representatives would hear all testimonies and discussions, gaining a complete understanding of the issues at hand. It would also hold legislators accountable for their participation and engagement in the legislative process.

Reducing Politicization and Grandstanding

Limiting the dissemination of hearings to transcripts would significantly reduce opportunities for political grandstanding. Without the visual and emotional impact of video, representatives would be less incentivized to use hearings as platforms for social media theatrics. Transcripts provide a more neutral and factual record of proceedings, encouraging a focus on substance over style. This shift would help restore the primary purpose of hearings: to investigate issues thoroughly and impartially.

Enhancing Legislative Effectiveness

With full attendance and a focus on detailed transcripts, legislative committees would likely become more effective in their fact-finding missions. Legislators would be better informed, having heard all testimonies and discussions, leading to more nuanced and well-rounded policy decisions. The reduced emphasis on performance would also encourage more thoughtful and productive dialogues among committee members and witnesses.

ADDRESSING POTENTIAL CONCERNS

Transparency and Public Trust

One might argue that limiting video recordings could reduce transparency and public trust in the legislative process. However, this concern can be mitigated by ensuring that transcripts are comprehensive, easily accessible, and promptly published. Detailed transcripts would still provide the public with a clear record of proceedings, maintaining transparency while removing the distractions of visual media.

Security Considerations

Video recordings should still be allowed for security purposes to ensure that there is a visual record in case of any disputes or incidents during hearings. This measure would maintain a balance between security needs and the reform's objectives.

CONCLUSION

Reforming the practices of public hearings in legislative committees to require full attendance by members and limiting dissemination to transcripts, except for security purposes, is a necessary step to restore the integrity and effectiveness of these important processes. The current exploitation of hearings for social media attention and fundraising undermines their primary purpose of fact-finding and informed decision-making. By implementing these changes, we can ensure that legislative hearings remain focused on uncovering the truth and crafting policies that genuinely serve the public interest.

Part III

❖

WARNINGS AGAINST THE MISCHIEFS OF FOREIGN INTRIGUE

He that passeth by, and meddleth with strife belonging not to him,
is like one that taketh a dog by the ears.

—PROVERBS 26:17 (KING JAMES VERSION)

IT IS IMPORTANT TO NOTE that this is the largest chapter in the book, underscoring the numerous theses derived from Washington's Farewell Address. This reflects the profound concern Washington had regarding the potential damage to a democratic republic if it engages in military adventurism abroad. His emphasis highlights the seriousness with which he viewed the risks of straying from a path of cautious and principled foreign policy.

THESIS 39

Observe good faith and justice toward all nations;
cultivate peace and harmony with all.

This maxim underscores the profound importance of upholding principles of fairness and equity in international relations.

Throughout the epochs, civilizations have grappled with the complexities of diplomacy and the pursuit of global harmony. From the empires of antiquity to the modern nation-states of the 21st century, the imperative of good faith and justice has remained central to the conduct of international affairs. Treaties, alliances, and diplomatic exchanges have sought to establish frameworks grounded in mutual respect and cooperation, recognizing the inherent interdependence of nations.

Consider, for instance, the Treaty of Westphalia, signed in 1648, which brought an end to the devastating Thirty Years' War in Europe. This landmark agreement introduced the concept of state sovereignty and laid the groundwork for a system of international relations based on principles of good faith and justice. By acknowledging the rights of individual states to govern their internal affairs, the treaty exemplified the importance of mutual respect and noninterference in diplomatic relations.

Similarly, the creation of the League of Nations after World War I represented a concerted effort to prevent future conflicts through collective security and diplomatic cooperation. Although ultimately flawed in its execution, the League embodied the aspirations of nations to uphold principles of fairness and equity on a global scale.

In the aftermath of World War II, the founding of the United Nations reaffirmed the commitment of member states to promote social progress, uphold human rights, and maintain international peace and security. Through its charter, the UN articulated a vision of a world guided by principles of good faith and justice, where disputes are resolved through dialogue and negotiation rather than resorting to violence.

In the 21st century, as the world grapples with an array of complex challenges—from climate change to terrorism—the imperative of good faith and justice remains as vital as ever. By fostering dialogue, cooperation, and respect for international law that does not violate our constitutional principles, we can cultivate an environment conducive to peace and stability. Through a steadfast commitment to these principles, we can transcend historical animosities and forge a future defined by peace, prosperity, and harmony while also ensuring a strong defensive posture keeps any military challengers at bay.

Washington's timeless observation serves as a beacon of moral guidance, reminding us of the enduring importance of upholding principles of good faith and justice in our interactions with other nations.

THESIS 40

Nothing is more essential than to shun passionate hatred against
particular nations and passionate attachments for other nations.

George Washington emphasized the importance of avoiding passionate hatred against particular nations and passionate attachments to others because he believed that such emotions could lead to unnecessary conflicts and entanglements that would threaten the young nation's stability and independence. This principle was a cornerstone of his foreign policy, which aimed at maintaining neutrality and avoiding entanglements in foreign alliances and wars.

Here are some historic examples from his presidency that illustrate his adherence to this principle:

1. NEUTRALITY PROCLAMATION OF 1793

During Washington's presidency, Europe was embroiled in conflicts, particularly the wars following the French Revolution. The United States faced pressure from both Britain and France to support their respective sides.

Washington issued the Neutrality Proclamation in 1793, declaring that the United States would remain neutral in the conflict between France and Great Britain. This proclamation was aimed at preventing the United States from being drawn into the wars of Europe.

By choosing neutrality, Washington demonstrated his commitment to avoiding "passionate attachments" to France, despite the nation's previous assistance during the American Revolutionary War, and "passionate hatred" toward Britain, despite their recent adversarial relationship.

2. JAY TREATY (1794)

Tensions were high between the United States and Great Britain due to issues such as British forts on American soil and the seizure of American ships.

Washington supported the Jay Treaty, negotiated by Chief Justice John Jay, which sought to resolve these issues and prevent war. The treaty was controversial and faced significant opposition, particularly from those who were pro-French.

The Jay Treaty was an example of Washington's efforts to avoid passionate hatred against Britain. Despite strong domestic opposition and the pro-French sentiment among many Americans, Washington prioritized a pragmatic approach to ensure peace and stability.

SUMMARY

Washington's emphasis on avoiding passionate hatred and attachments was rooted in his desire to protect the fledgling nation from the perils of foreign entanglements. By maintaining neutrality and focusing on American interests, he sought to ensure that the United States could grow and prosper without being drawn into the conflicts of other nations. His actions during his presidency, including the Neutrality Proclamation, the Jay Treaty, and his Farewell Address, all reflect this guiding principle.

Here are some examples of how neglecting George Washington's maxim about avoiding passionate hatred and attachments in foreign policy has caused problems for the United States:

1. VIETNAM WAR (1955–1975)

The United States became heavily involved in Vietnam to counter the spread of communism, driven by a passionate attachment to the idea of containing communism and supporting friendly governments worldwide.

The Vietnam War resulted in significant loss of life, substantial financial cost, and deep political and social divisions within the United States. The passionate attachment to fighting communism led to a prolonged conflict that ultimately ended in withdrawal and failure to achieve its goals. A tragic irony for those dedicated service members whose names are carved into the Vietnam memorial, we as Americans now freely travel and trade with Vietnam, highlighting the futility of the conflict.

The Vietnam War exemplifies how a passionate attachment to an ideological struggle can lead to extensive involvement in a conflict with long-term detrimental consequences for the nation.

2. IRAN-CONTRA AFFAIR (1980S)

During the Reagan administration, the United States was involved in a covert operation that involved selling arms to Iran (despite an arms embargo) and using the proceeds to fund Contra rebels in Nicaragua.

This affair led to a major political scandal, damaging the credibility of the U.S. government and leading to legal and political repercussions for those involved.

The Iran-Contra Affair highlighted the dangers of clandestine operations driven by passionate attachments to certain groups or outcomes, undermining the rule of law and damaging international relations.

3. IRAQ WAR (2003–2011)

The U.S. invasion of Iraq was driven by the belief that Iraq possessed weapons of mass destruction (WMDs) and the desire to remove Saddam Hussein from power, partially fueled by a passionate reaction to the 9/11 terrorist attacks.

The Iraq War resulted in prolonged conflict, significant loss of life, substantial financial costs, and regional instability. The intelligence about WMDs was later found to be inaccurate, leading to widespread criticism of the war. Additionally, the Iraq War served as a diversion from the legitimate conflict in Afghanistan, where the primary focus should have been on dismantling al-Qaeda and stabilizing the region.

The Iraq War demonstrates how passionate reactions to perceived threats can lead to major military interventions with long-lasting and often negative consequences for regional and global stability. The diversion of resources and attention from Afghanistan further complicated efforts to achieve stability and success in the war against terrorism.

4. U.S.-RUSSIA RELATIONS POST-COLD WAR

Since the end of the Cold War, U.S. relations with Russia have often been marked by a mix of animosity and strategic competition. This has included issues such as NATO expansion, election interference, and conflicts in Ukraine and Syria.

Tensions have led to sanctions, proxy conflicts, and a general deterioration in diplomatic relations, contributing to global instability and complicating efforts to address shared challenges like terrorism.

5. U.S.-IRAN RELATIONS (UPDATED MAY 2026)

The current animosity between the United States and Iran did not begin in a vacuum. It began with the 1953 coup against Prime Minister Mohammad Mosaddegh, carried out with the involvement of the CIA and British intelligence, and it hardened after the 1979 Iranian Revolution and the hostage crisis, when 52 American diplomats and citizens were held for 444 days. From that moment forward, distrust became the default posture between the two nations.

For decades, this antagonism has manifested through sanctions, diplomatic isolation, covert operations, proxy conflicts, and military confrontations.

But the events of 2025 and 2026 have revealed the catastrophic danger of allowing that hostility to become national policy without wisdom, restraint, or historical understanding.

Upon returning to office, President Trump restored his "maximum pressure" campaign against Iran in February 2025, directing sanctions enforcement, pressure on Iran's oil exports, and a renewed effort to deny Iran nuclear and missile capabilities. Negotiations followed, but by June 2025, talks gave way to the so-called Twelve-Day War, during which the U.S. struck Iranian nuclear infrastructure. By February 28, 2026, the United States and Israel had launched a much larger military operation against Iran, targeting military assets and top leadership, and the conflict widened into a regional war.

What should concern every American is not merely that force was used, but the manner in which it was justified. The rhetoric surrounding Iran has too often drifted from condemnation of a regime into demonization of Islam and dehumanization of the Iranian people themselves. When threats are made against civilian infrastructure—energy systems, ports, and even desalination facilities—the moral line between opposing a government and punishing a people begins to disappear.

This is precisely the danger Washington warned against: passionate hatred replacing sober judgment.

Compounding this danger is the ever-present fear of nuclear weapons. That fear is legitimate. A nuclear-armed Iran would alter the balance of power in the Middle East and present real strategic risks. But fear, when left unchecked, has a way of distorting judgment. It has driven policymakers into an all-or-nothing mentality, one that assumes only two outcomes: total capitulation or total confrontation. Lost in this binary thinking is the disciplined work of nuanced risk assessment and cost analysis. What are the second- and third-order consequences of military action? What are the risks of escalation across a region already on edge? What are the economic and human costs of disruption to global energy markets? And, perhaps most importantly, what are the long-term consequences of closing off avenues for internal reform within Iran itself?

By allowing nuclear fear to dominate strategic thinking, policymakers risk replacing prudence with urgency, and wisdom with reaction.

The tragedy is that America has had another path available. During the Cold War, the United States did not defeat the Soviet system by convincing the Russian people that we hated them or by dropping bombs on Moscow. We cultivated hope. We projected confidence in liberty, free expression, constitutional government, religious freedom, and the dignity of the individual. We made it clear that our quarrel was with tyranny, not with the people trapped beneath it.

Iran presents a similar missed opportunity. Its population is young, educated, culturally rich, and filled with people who have repeatedly shown courage in demanding dignity and freedom. Yet instead of cultivating moderate, reform-minded Iranians who might see in the American system a model of ordered liberty, our policy too often collapses Iran into a single enemy image. That mistake strengthens hardliners, feeds propaganda, and teaches ordinary Iranians that America's promise of liberty may not apply to them.

The current war has also exposed the danger of insular decision-making. A republic should not stumble into war through a narrow circle of loyalists, ideological warriors, and political performers. Decisions of war and peace require consultation with allies, Congress, military professionals, regional experts, diplomats, historians, and those who understand Iranian society beyond caricature. Yet the administration's approach has often appeared isolated from allied caution and historical expertise.

At the heart of this failure lies an old assumption: that we are better than them and therefore knowing them does not matter. That assumption has haunted American foreign policy from Vietnam to Iraq. It blinds leaders to culture, memory, religion, pride, grievance, and aspiration. It mistakes superior power for superior understanding.

The antagonistic relationship with Iran exemplifies how sustained animosity can entrench conflict and prevent constructive engagement. By focusing solely on the Iranian government and its actions, the United States risks alienating a significant portion of the Iranian population that could be instrumental in fostering long-term change. This neglect can perpetuate cycles of hostility, strengthen authoritarian forces, and make peace more difficult with every passing year.

Neglecting George Washington's advice about avoiding passionate hatreds and attachments has repeatedly led the United States into costly foreign policy disasters. From Vietnam to Iraq, from Iran-Contra to the current war with Iran, emotional and ideological commitments have driven decisions whose consequences far outlast the leaders who made them. Washington's call for a measured, interest-based, morally disciplined foreign policy remains not merely relevant, but existential.

THESIS 41

In place of these extreme passions, just and amicable
feelings toward all should be created.

Throughout the annals of time, humanity has been ensnared in the throes of passionate hatred and fervent attachments toward particular nations. From the ancient rivalries of empires vying for supremacy to the ideological conflicts of the modern era, the consequences of unchecked animosity have been profound and far-reaching. The Peloponnesian War, with its tragic aftermath of devastation and ruin, serves as a stark reminder of the perils of unrestrained hostility and the urgent need for dialogue and reconciliation.

In the modern era, the specter of ideological confrontation loomed large during the Cold War, casting a shadow of fear and uncertainty over the global landscape. The bitter rivalry between superpowers threatened to plunge the world into the abyss of nuclear annihilation, underscoring the imperative of dialogue and cooperation in averting catastrophe. It was through the cultivation of just and amicable relations that the icy tensions gradually thawed, paving the way for détente and the eventual end of the Cold War.

Today, as the world grapples with an array of complex challenges, Washington's admonition resonates with renewed urgency. In an age marked by rising nationalism, xenophobia, and geopolitical tensions, the imperative of fostering equitable diplomacy has never been more pressing. Leaders must heed Washington's counsel and prioritize dialogue, cooperation, and empathy in their interactions with other nations.

In the realm of international relations, there exist shining examples of nations transcending historical animosities to forge enduring partnerships based on mutual respect and cooperation. The reconciliation between former adversaries such as France and Germany stand as a testament to the transformative power of reconciliation and dialogue. Similarly, the recent diplomatic breakthroughs between traditional rivals like Israel and Saudi Arabia offer hope for a future where dialogue triumphs over discord and cooperation prevails over conflict.

By embracing Washington's vision of nurturing equitable diplomacy, leaders can chart a course toward a world where justice, fairness, and mutual respect serve as the cornerstones of international relations. In doing so, they honor the wisdom of America's founding father and pave the way for a more harmonious and prosperous future for our children.

THESIS 42

The nation which indulges toward another a habitual hatred or a habitual fondness is a habitual target of others.

Washington's timeless observation underscores the critical importance of maintaining balanced and measured relations with other nations, as extreme sentiments can make a nation vulnerable to exploitation and hostility from others.

In his insightful observation, Washington highlights a fundamental truth about international relations—one that has reverberated through history and continues to resonate in contemporary geopolitics. The notion that a nation's indulgence in either intense animosity or unwavering affection toward another can render it vulnerable to exploitation by opportunistic adversaries is a sobering reminder of the perils of extreme and reactionary sentiments. We now use the term "blowback" to define these reactions.

RISE OF THE KHMER ROUGE (1975)

During the Vietnam War, the U.S. conducted extensive bombing campaigns in Cambodia to disrupt North Vietnamese supply lines and bases. This bombing campaign caused widespread destruction and instability in Cambodia.

The devastation and chaos resulting from the bombings contributed to the rise of the Khmer Rouge, a radical communist movement led by Pol Pot. The Khmer Rouge capitalized on the social and political upheaval, eventually taking control of Cambodia in 1975. They then carried out one of the most brutal genocides of the 20th century, resulting in the deaths of an estimated 1.7 to 2 million people.

The rise of the Khmer Rouge illustrates how U.S. military actions in one country can have catastrophic effects on another. The indirect consequences of the bombing campaign in Cambodia highlight the dangers of passionate and aggressive foreign policies, emphasizing the need for caution and consideration of long-term impacts.

IRANIAN HOSTAGE CRISIS (1979–1981)

As stated earlier, the U.S. support for the Shah of Iran, who was widely viewed as a repressive dictator by many Iranians, led to significant animosity. In 1953, the CIA orchestrated a coup to overthrow the democratically elected Prime Minister Mohammad Mossadegh and reinstate the Shah, which created long-lasting resentment.

The culmination of this animosity was the Iranian Revolution in 1979, which saw the Shah overthrown and replaced by an Islamic Republic led by Ayatollah Khomeini. In retaliation against perceived American interference and support for the Shah, Iranian militants stormed the U.S. Embassy in Tehran and took 52 American hostages, holding them for 444 days. This crisis severely damaged U.S.-Iran relations and has led to decades of enmity and conflict between the two nations.

9/11 TERRORIST ATTACKS (2001)

The U.S. military presence in the Middle East, particularly in Saudi Arabia, and its support for authoritarian regimes in the region fueled anti-American sentiments among groups that grew extremist in light of frustrated attempts to effect change in their own societies.

These policies contributed to the radicalization of groups like al-Qaeda, which saw the U.S. as a primary enemy. The most devastating act of blowback was the September 11, 2001 terrorist attacks, where al-Qaeda operatives hijacked commercial airliners and carried out coordinated attacks on the World Trade Center and the Pentagon, resulting in nearly 3,000 deaths. This event drastically reshaped U.S. foreign policy and led to the War on Terror, including prolonged conflicts in Afghanistan and Iraq.

RISE OF ISIS (2014)

The U.S. invasion of Iraq in 2003 and the subsequent dismantling of the Iraqi military and government institutions created a power vacuum and widespread instability. The mistreatment of Sunni populations and former Ba'athists further exacerbated sectarian tensions.

These conditions facilitated the rise of extremist groups, most notably ISIS (Islamic State of Iraq and Syria). ISIS capitalized on the chaos to seize large territories in Iraq and Syria, declaring a caliphate and conducting widespread atrocities. The group also inspired and orchestrated terrorist attacks globally, directly challenging U.S. interests and security.

AFGHANISTAN AND THE TALIBAN (1980S–PRESENT)

During the 1980s, the U.S. supported Afghan mujahideen fighters against the Soviet Union, providing them with arms and training. However, after the Soviet withdrawal, the U.S. largely disengaged from Afghanistan, leaving a fragmented and war-torn nation.

The power vacuum and lack of stability allowed the Taliban to rise to power in the 1990s, providing a safe haven for al-Qaeda. This connection led directly to the 9/11 attacks and the subsequent U.S. invasion of Afghanistan. Despite years of conflict and efforts to rebuild the country, the Taliban's resurgence and eventual return to power in 2021 demonstrate the long-term consequences of initial U.S. policies and disengagement.

George Washington's advice to avoid passionate hatred and attachments in foreign policy remains profoundly relevant. The examples of blowback from adversaries like Iran, al-Qaeda, ISIS, and the Taliban illustrate how mistreatment and passionate antagonism can lead to severe and long-lasting repercussions. These cases underscore the importance of measured, interest-based foreign policy that seeks to understand and address the underlying causes of animosity rather than exacerbating them through reactionary measures.

THESIS 43

An addictive sympathy for a favorite nation lures our nation into
participation in the quarrels and wars without adequate justification.

Washington's caution regarding an addictive sympathy for a favorite nation, as highlighted in his observation, underscores the dangers inherent in cultivating unwarranted favoritism toward other nations. This profound insight illuminates the perilous path that nations may tread when lured into participation in the quarrels and wars of favored nations without adequate justification. Such sentiments, left unchecked, can entangle a nation in conflicts that do not serve its best interests.

Throughout history, we have witnessed numerous examples of nations falling prey to the allure of excessive national affection. One such instance occurred during the early years of the United States, when passionate attachments to European powers threatened to embroil the young nation in the conflicts of the Old World. The temptation to align with one nation over another often clouded judgment, leading to decisions that compromised America's sovereignty and integrity.

The War of 1812 serves as a poignant illustration of the consequences of succumbing to addictive sympathy for a favorite nation. Fueled by fervent support for Britain or France, factions within the United States clamored for involvement in the ongoing European conflicts. Despite warnings against entangling alliances, partisan interests prevailed, pushing the nation toward a costly and divisive war.

Similarly, the period leading up to World War I witnessed the dangers of unabated national affection. As tensions escalated between rival European powers, the United States found itself torn between its traditional policy of neutrality and the pressures of sentimentality toward certain nations. In the end, misguided alliances and fervent loyalties dragged the nation into a global conflict, resulting in unimaginable loss and suffering.

In the modern era, this dynamic has not disappeared. The United States maintains close and often justified relationships with key allies, including long-standing support for nations such as Israel. While such alliances can serve legitimate strategic and moral purposes, they also carry the inherent risk Washington warned against that sympathy can evolve into unquestioned alignment. When this occurs, the line between defending shared interests and inheriting another nation's conflicts can become dangerously blurred. The challenge is not the alliance itself, but the loss of independent judgment that may follow when policy is driven more by loyalty than by clear-eyed assessment of American interests. This dynamic will be explored in greater detail in subsequent chapters.

The tendency to align with a favored nation blinds us to the complexities of international relations and undermines our ability to act in our own best interests. Instead of succumbing to emotional attachments, we must approach foreign affairs with a clear-eyed realism, guided by a steadfast commitment to our nation's welfare.

As we navigate the complexities of the modern world, we must heed Washington's wisdom and guard against the allure of sentimental attachments that may lead us astray. Only by maintaining a prudent and principled approach to foreign relations can we ensure the security and prosperity of our nation for generations to come.

THESIS 44

Concessions and privileges to a favorite nation denied to others is apt to create an atmosphere of jealousy, ill-will, and a disposition to retaliate.

George Washington's warning about granting concessions and privileges to a favorite nation, while denying them to others, is highly relevant to the recent history of U.S.-Russia relations. Here are a few key points that illustrate this dynamic:

1. NATO EXPANSION

Since the end of the Cold War, NATO has expanded significantly, incorporating many Eastern European countries that were once part of the Soviet sphere of influence. This expansion has often been perceived by Russia as a direct threat to its security and sphere of influence.

Russia has viewed NATO's eastward expansion as a form of favoritism toward Western-aligned countries, creating a sense of encirclement and exclusion. This perception has fueled resentment and suspicion toward the West, exacerbating tensions.

In response, Russia has taken steps to assert its influence in its near abroad. This includes actions such as the annexation of Crimea in 2014 and support for separatists in Eastern Ukraine, which can be seen as retaliatory measures aimed at countering what it perceives as Western encroachment.

2. Economic Sanctions and Diplomatic Isolation

Following various actions by Russia, including the annexation of Crimea and perceived interference in the 2016 U.S. presidential election, the United States and its allies have imposed a series of economic sanctions on Russia.

The sanctions have been viewed by Russia as punitive measures that unfairly target its economy and political leadership. This has led to increased anti-Western sentiment within Russia and bolstered the government's narrative of a Western conspiracy to weaken the country.

In retaliation, Russia has implemented its own counter-sanctions and has taken steps to deepen its alliances with non-Western countries, such as China and Iran. Additionally, Russia has engaged in various forms of asymmetric warfare, including cyberattacks and disinformation campaigns against Western countries.

3. Support for Rival States and Entities

The U.S. has provided significant support to countries and entities that are opposed to Russian interests, such as Ukraine and various NATO member states.

The Maidan Revolution, also known as the Euromaidan protests, began in late 2013 and culminated in early 2014 with the ousting of Ukraine's pro-Russian president, Viktor Yanukovych. The protests were sparked by Yanukovych's decision to reject an association agreement with the European Union in favor of closer ties with Russia, which led to widespread demonstrations advocating for European integration and governmental reforms.

From Russia's viewpoint, the Maidan Revolution was seen as a Western-orchestrated plot designed to pull Ukraine out of its sphere of influence and integrate it into Western institutions such as the EU and NATO. The significant involvement of Western diplomats and politicians, who were seen offering support to the protesters and criticizing Yanukovych's government, fueled this perception.

Russia interpreted the West's open support for the protesters, including visits by high-profile Western politicians like John McCain, to the Maidan Square, as evidence of direct interference in Ukraine's internal affairs. Additionally, U.S. aid and the presence of numerous Western NGOs in Ukraine were perceived by Russia as mechanisms for fostering pro-Western sentiments and destabilizing the pro-Russian government.

Russian state media and government officials propagated the narrative that the Maidan Revolution was a coup d'état backed by Western powers. This narrative emphasized the involvement of Western intelligence agencies and suggested that the revolution was part of a broader strategy to encircle Russia and diminish its influence in Eastern Europe.

The perception of the Maidan Revolution as a Western plot significantly worsened U.S.-Russia relations. It reinforced Russia's fears of Western encroachment and increased its sense of strategic vulnerability. The subsequent Western support for the new Ukrainian government, including economic aid and military assistance, further entrenched this animosity.

In retaliation, Russia annexed Crimea in 2014 and supported separatist movements in Eastern Ukraine, actions that were justified by Russia as necessary to protect ethnic Russians and Russian speakers from an illegitimate, Western-backed regime. These moves have led to ongoing conflict and instability in the region, demonstrating the long-term repercussions of perceived favoritism and intervention.

George Washington's advice about the dangers of granting concessions and privileges to a favorite nation while denying them to others can be seen in the context of U.S.-Russia relations. NATO expansion, economic sanctions, and selective support have all contributed to an atmosphere of jealousy, ill will, and a strong disposition to retaliate on Russia's part. These actions have led to a cycle of antagonism and countermeasures, illustrating the ongoing relevance of Washington's insights into foreign policy dynamics.

4. THE UNITED STATES AND ISRAEL

In the modern era, few relationships better illustrate the complexity—and potential danger—of habitual fondness than that between the United States and Israel. This relationship is rooted in both strategic considerations and deeply human sympathies that emerged in the aftermath of World War II.

The horrors inflicted upon the Jewish people during the Holocaust left an indelible mark on the conscience of the world, and particularly on the American people. For many Americans—especially within evangelical Christian communities—support for Israel has been shaped not only by geopolitical interests but by moral conviction, historical memory, and religious belief. These sentiments have fostered a natural and enduring sympathy for the Jewish people and their right to a secure homeland.

Since Israel's founding in 1948, the United States has played a central role in its development and security. Through diplomatic recognition, economic assistance, military aid, and strategic cooperation, America has helped ensure Israel's survival in a hostile regional environment. This support has often been justified, both morally and strategically, as Israel has faced existential threats from neighboring states and nonstate actors.

Yet Washington's warning is not concerned with whether an alliance is justified at its origin, but whether it remains disciplined over time.

The strength of the U.S.–Israel relationship has, at times, evolved into a level of alignment that risks blurring the distinction between shared interests and inherited conflicts. American support—political, military, and diplomatic— has provided Israel with a degree of latitude in its regional actions that is not afforded to many other nations. This has included military operations and strategic decisions that carry significant consequences not only for Israel, but for regional stability and, by extension, for American interests.

The cost of this alignment has not been insignificant. The United States has, at times, borne diplomatic strain with allies, increased hostility from adversaries, and entanglement in regional conflicts that are not always directly tied to core American interests. More importantly, it has contributed to a broader perception that American policy in the region is not guided by consistent principles, but by preferential treatment.

At the same time, it is essential to recognize a critical distinction: the government of Israel and the people of Israel are not one and the same. Like any nation, Israel contains a diverse population with a wide range of political views, moral perspectives, and visions for its future. The actions of a more short-term governing coalition do not fully represent the more long-term will or character of its citizens. This distinction is vital if one is to maintain both intellectual honesty and moral clarity.

Today, the relationship faces a new and profound challenge. While Israel's right to exist as a sovereign nation is well established and broadly supported, the question of how that right is extended—or denied—to others beyond its borders has become increasingly central. The long-standing conflict over Arab self-determination in occupied territories raises difficult questions about sovereignty, security, and human dignity that cannot be ignored without consequence.

None of this negates the legitimacy of a U.S.–Israel alliance. Rather, it underscores the necessity of maintaining independence of judgment within it.

Washington's warning reminds us that even the most justified alliances can become liabilities when they evolve into unquestioned loyalty. A republic must retain the ability to evaluate each situation on its own merits, guided not by sentiment or habit, but by principle, prudence, and a clear understanding of its own national interest.

THESIS 45

These concessions allow ambitious and corrupt citizens who devote themselves to the favorite nation substantial prejudice to betray and sacrifice the interests of their own country in exchange for short-term popularity rooted in the vices of ambition, corruption, or infatuation.

CHINA AND ECONOMIC ENGAGEMENT

Over the past few decades, U.S. engagement with China has focused on economic integration and trade, with the expectation that economic liberalization would lead to political liberalization.

Some U.S. business leaders and politicians have been accused of turning a blind eye to China's human rights abuses, intellectual property theft, and unfair trade practices in favor of short-term economic gains. This includes lobbying for policies that benefit from the lucrative Chinese market.

This approach has led to significant trade imbalances, loss of manufacturing jobs in the U.S., and a growing strategic rivalry as China has not only failed to democratize but also become more authoritarian and assertive on the global stage. The focus on short-term economic benefits has arguably compromised long-term strategic interests.

SAUDI ARABIA AND OIL DEPENDENCE

The U.S. has maintained a close relationship with Saudi Arabia, largely due to its vast oil reserves and strategic importance in the Middle East.

U.S. officials and business leaders have often been accused of overlooking Saudi Arabia's human rights violations, including the treatment of women and political dissidents, in favor of maintaining strong bilateral relations and securing energy supplies. Though the 9/11 attackers were all from Saudi Arabia, radicalized by the indigenous brand of Wahhabi Islam, and there were suspicions of some government support of al Qaeda, our nation's leadership did not hold Saudi Arabia as accountable as many thought it should.

U.S. SUPPORT FOR LATIN AMERICAN DICTATORSHIPS

During the Cold War, the U.S. supported various authoritarian regimes in Latin America, such as those in Chile, Argentina, and Nicaragua, to counter perceived communist threats.

Some U.S. politicians and officials supported these regimes, often for personal or ideological reasons, despite their human rights abuses and corruption. This support was sometimes driven by a desire for short-term strategic gains against Soviet influence.

The Dulles brothers, John Foster Dulles and Allen Dulles, played pivotal roles in undermining Central American governments during the 1950s to benefit American corporations such as the United Fruit Company. John Foster Dulles, as Secretary of State, and Allen Dulles, as Director of the CIA, orchestrated covert operations that toppled democratically elected governments perceived as threats to American business interests. A notable example is the 1954 coup in Guatemala, where the CIA orchestrated the overthrow of President Jacobo Árbenz, whose land reforms threatened United Fruit's vast holdings. This intervention was framed as a fight against communism, but it primarily served to protect corporate profits, leading to decades of instability and repression in the region. The Dulles brothers' actions exemplify how U.S. foreign policy was manipulated to serve the interests of powerful American companies at the expense of local populations in Latin America.

This policy led to widespread human suffering and anti-American sentiment in the region, undermining the U.S.'s moral authority and long-term interests. The legacy of this favoritism has left lasting scars on U.S.-Latin American relations and continues to affect perceptions of American foreign policy in the region.

POLITICAL INCENTIVES AND THE U.S.–ISRAEL RELATIONSHIP

Beyond strategy and history, the relationship between the United States and Israel is shaped by powerful domestic political forces that illustrate Washington's warning. For many American leaders—particularly those supported by evangelical constituencies—support for Israel is influenced not only by national security considerations, but by deeply held religious beliefs. In some cases, interpretations of scripture elevate Israel's security to a matter of moral or even divine obligation. While sincerely held, such convictions exist outside the realm of secular statecraft grounded in reasoned judgment and national interest.

This dynamic is reinforced by organized political advocacy. Groups such as the American Israel Public Affairs Committee have effectively cultivated broad bipartisan support through sustained engagement, policy influence, and campaign backing. The result is a political environment in which strong alignment with Israel often brings electoral, financial, and media advantages, while dissent—however measured—can carry real political cost.

In today's media landscape, these incentives are amplified. Public officials who offer unequivocal support are often rewarded with visibility and approval, creating a feedback loop that discourages nuance and reinforces uniformity. Over time, this can shift policy from independent evaluation to reflexive alignment.

The issue is not the legitimacy of the alliance, but the erosion of judgment. When religious conviction, political incentive, and organized advocacy converge, policymakers risk placing the perceived interests of a favored nation above a disciplined assessment of their own. Washington's warning remains clear: friendship must never become subordination.

George Washington's warning about the dangers of favoritism in foreign policy is reflected in these historic examples, where ambitious and corrupt citizens prioritized the interests of a favored nation over the broader interests of the United States. Whether in the Middle East, East Asia, or Latin

America, such actions have often led to significant long-term consequences, including strained international relations, economic imbalances, and damage to the U.S.'s global reputation. These examples underscore the importance of a balanced and principled approach to foreign policy.

THESIS 46

The great rule for us regarding foreign nations is in extending our commercial relations with as little political connection as possible.

Throughout the ages, nations have grappled with the complexities of foreign policy, often oscillating between the pursuit of economic prosperity and the pitfalls of political alliances. Washington's insight serves as a timeless reminder of the importance of prioritizing commercial ties while minimizing the risks associated with excessive political involvement.

One poignant example of the significance of this principle can be found in the mercantilist policies of colonial empires during the Age of Exploration. European powers, driven by the desire for economic dominance, established far-reaching trade networks and exploited overseas territories for their resources. However, the entanglement of economic interests with political agendas often led to conflicts and power struggles among rival colonial powers.

Similarly, the emergence of globalization in the modern era has ushered in unprecedented opportunities for economic cooperation and exchange. The proliferation of free trade agreements and the expansion of multinational corporations have transformed the global economy, fostering prosperity and innovation. Yet the interdependence created by economic globalization has also exposed nations to vulnerabilities, as evidenced by the ripple effects of financial crises and trade disputes.

In recent history, the Cold War exemplified the dangers of allowing political ideologies to dictate economic relationships. The ideological rivalry between the United States and the Soviet Union divided the world into competing spheres of influence, fueling proxy conflicts and geopolitical tensions. The intertwining of economic and political interests underscored the need for nations to exercise caution in navigating foreign relations.

Moreover, the rise of economic nationalism and protectionism in the post-Cold War era has further complicated the relationship between commerce and politics. Issues such as trade imbalances, intellectual property rights, and market access have become flashpoints in international relations, leading to diplomatic standoffs and tariff wars.

International trade agreements with countries whose political systems may not align with our democratic ideals can play a crucial role in fostering prosperity and gradual political change. By engaging in trade, these countries experience economic growth, which can improve the standard of living for their citizens and create a more prosperous society. This economic interdependence not only brings material benefits but also exposes the local population to the principles of a free market and democratic values. Over time, as citizens witness the advantages of economic freedom and prosperity, they may become more inclined to advocate for political reforms and greater personal liberties. Trade can thus serve as a catalyst for change, encouraging governments to adopt more open and democratic practices to maintain economic growth and stability. This approach underscores the power of economic engagement in promoting long-term positive transformations within nations that may initially seem resistant to democratic ideals.

THESIS 47

Excessive partiality for one foreign nation and excessive dislike of another cause us to see danger only on one side and serve to hide, and even increase, a more negative influence from the other.

Washington's sagacious observation on foreign relations underscores the enduring importance of maintaining impartiality and balance in diplomatic endeavors.

Throughout history, nations have grappled with the challenge of navigating the intricate web of global politics while balancing competing interests and alliances. However, the tendency toward excessive partiality for certain nations and disdain for others has often clouded judgment and hindered the pursuit of peaceful resolutions to conflicts.

One compelling example of the perils of biased diplomacy can be observed in the lead-up to World War I. The system of entangling alliances that characterized European politics at the time led to a situation where nations were bound by commitments to their allies, regardless of the merit or justice of their cause. This web of alliances, coupled with nationalist fervor and imperial ambitions, ultimately culminated in a catastrophic global conflict that claimed millions of lives.

Similarly, the Cold War era saw the proliferation of ideological rivalries and superpower competition, with the United States and the Soviet Union vying for influence on the world stage. The policy of containment, championed by American policymakers, sought to curb the spread of communism through a combination of military intervention and strategic alliances. However, this approach often led to the support of authoritarian regimes and covert operations that undermined democratic principles and fueled anti-American sentiment in various parts of the world.

Furthermore, the post-9/11 landscape has been characterized by the global war on terror and the proliferation of unilateral military interventions under the guise of national security. The vilification of certain nations and the promotion of interventionist policies have perpetuated cycles of violence and instability in regions such as the Middle East, exacerbating humanitarian crises and breeding resentment toward the United States.

THESIS 48

With neutrality we would be more highly respected so that belligerent nations, under the impossibility of taking advantage of us, will not lightly risk giving us provocation.

By abstaining from entangling alliances and refraining from involvement in foreign conflicts, neutral states position themselves as impartial arbiters committed to upholding stability and noninterference.

All that said, as a neutral state, America must maintain a robust defense capability ensuring that as a neutral nation it can protect its territorial integrity, political independence, and international shipping. This, along with the military training and state guard service expressed in Thesis 64, will enable our country to resist external pressures and interventions, allowing it to uphold its neutral stance and global trade without succumbing to coercion.

THESIS 49

Take care always to keep ourselves on a respectable defensive posture; we may safely trust temporary alliances for extraordinary emergencies.

Nations that have prioritized defensive strategies over aggressive expansionism have often emerged as resilient and esteemed entities on the global stage. By concentrating on fortifying their defenses and safeguarding their sovereignty, these countries have effectively countered external threats and preserved their independence amidst challenging circumstances. For example, the defensive tactics employed by ancient civilizations like Rome enabled them to withstand external pressures and assert their influence across vast territories.

Furthermore, the maintenance of a defensive posture enables nations to cultivate alliances grounded in mutual interests and shared values, thereby enhancing their security and diplomatic efficacy. Temporary alliances formed during extraordinary crises, such as wartime coalitions and defense pacts, empower nations to pool their resources and confront common adversaries collectively. The alliances forged during World War II, such as the Allied Powers, exemplify the effectiveness of coordinated defensive measures in countering totalitarian aggression and upholding democratic principles.

By investing in modern defense capabilities and fostering strategic partnerships, countries can deter aggression, promote regional stability, and uphold international norms effectively. Organizations like the North Atlantic Treaty Organization (NATO) exemplify the value of collective defense arrangements in safeguarding member states against a specific external threat from the Soviet Union and preserving peace in the Euro-Atlantic region. However, the continued existence of this "defensive" alliance decades after the dissolution of the "aggressive" Soviet Union has contributed to the institutionalization of a perpetual state of conflict with its successor state, Russia.

THESIS 50

There can be no greater error than to expect or calculate upon real favors from nation to nation. It is an illusion, which experience should cure, which a just pride should discard.

Washington's observation holds significant implications for international relations. This thesis aims to explore the significance of this principle by examining historical examples and offering a detailed historical context to create a compelling narrative.

Throughout history, nations have often engaged in diplomatic relations and alliances with the expectation of receiving significant favors or concessions from their counterparts. However, experience has repeatedly shown that such expectations are often misguided and can lead to disappointment and resentment. The annals of history are replete with instances where nations entered into treaties or agreements with lofty expectations, only to find themselves betrayed or manipulated for the benefit of the other party.

For instance, the Treaty of Versailles, signed at the end of World War I, was hailed as a landmark agreement that would bring lasting peace and prosperity to Europe. However, the punitive terms imposed on Germany, coupled with the failure to address underlying grievances and inequalities, sowed the seeds of resentment and laid the groundwork for the rise of totalitarian regimes and the outbreak of World War II. This historical episode serves as a poignant reminder of the perils of expecting genuine favors or goodwill from other nations without considering their self-interests and motivations.

Furthermore, the principle espoused by Washington underscores the importance of maintaining a sense of realism and pragmatism in international relations. While diplomacy and cooperation between nations are essential for addressing common challenges and advancing shared goals, it is naive to expect altruistic behavior or benevolent gestures from states solely based on goodwill or friendship. Nations are driven by their national interests, which often prioritize self-preservation, security, and prosperity above all else.

Moreover, the observation highlights the significance of cultivating a sense of pride and self-reliance in national affairs. Relying too heavily on the benevolence of other nations can undermine a country's sovereignty and independence, making it susceptible to exploitation or coercion. Instead, nations should prioritize building their own strengths, capabilities, and resilience to navigate the complexities of the international arena effectively.

THESIS 51

Let existing alliances be observed in their genuine sense. But it would be unwise to extend them.

Washington's observation, reflected in the principle outlined in Thesis 13, advises the observation of existing alliances in their authentic context while cautioning against their extension, holds significant implications for international relations.

Throughout history, alliances have played a pivotal role in shaping the course of nations' interactions on the global stage. From ancient military pacts to modern-day diplomatic agreements, alliances have often been instrumental in securing strategic advantages, fostering cooperation, and maintaining stability among nations. However, the prudent management of these alliances is essential to prevent unintended consequences and ensure the preservation of national interests.

One of the key insights offered by this thesis is the importance of discerning the genuine essence of existing alliances. While alliances may initially serve to bolster mutual defense or promote economic cooperation, their extension beyond their original purpose can lead to unforeseen complications and entanglements. History is replete with examples of alliances that, once extended beyond their intended scope, resulted in unintended conflicts and strained relations between nations.

To follow up from Thesis 48 regarding the formation of NATO: when the Warsaw Pact dissolved in 1991, marking the end of the Cold War, it arguably signaled a unique opportunity for NATO to also conclude its mission and dissolve. NATO, originally established as a military alliance to counter Soviet influence, became a quasi-state entity that countries felt compelled to join, rather than a traditional treaty among friendly nations. Instead of disbanding, NATO expanded eastward, creating new security dilemmas and perpetuating a climate of suspicion and rivalry with Russia. The continuation and expansion of NATO post-Cold War transformed it into an institutional fixture that outlasted its original purpose, fostering tensions instead of facilitating a new era of cooperative security in Europe. Similarly, in the realm of economic alliances, the expansion of trade agreements without due consideration for their long-term implications can undermine domestic industries and compromise national sovereignty. The history of trade alliances is replete with instances where hastily negotiated agreements led to job losses, economic imbalances, and social upheaval within participating nations. An appropriate example for my home state of South Carolina was the North American Free Trade Agreement (NAFTA) that led to the destruction of upcountry cotton mills as many mill owners shut down their domestic production and fled to cheaper labor in Mexico, causing tremendous job losses in dozens of communities that had relied on those mills for generations.

THESIS 52

Harmony and liberal intercourse with all nations, are recommended by policy, humanity, and interest.

Washington's astute observation, advocating for harmony and liberal intercourse with all nations, resonates deeply with the essence of international diplomacy. This chapter aims to delve into the significance of Washington's principle, examining its relevance in historical contexts and contemporary diplomatic affairs.

Throughout history, nations have experienced the consequences of both harmonious and discordant relations with other states. Harmony and liberal intercourse, characterized by mutual respect, cooperation, and open dialogue, have often led to greater stability, economic prosperity, and cultural exchange among nations. Conversely, instances of hostility, isolationism, or protectionism have frequently resulted in conflict, economic downturns, and cultural stagnation.

Washington's emphasis on harmony and liberal intercourse aligns with fundamental principles of diplomacy, including policy, humanity, and mutual interest. By engaging in respectful dialogue and fostering mutual understanding, nations can address common challenges such as climate change, terrorism, and global health crises more effectively. Furthermore, promoting liberal trade policies and facilitating cultural exchanges can enhance economic growth, social development, and intercultural appreciation on a global scale.

However, achieving harmony and liberal intercourse in international relations requires concerted efforts from all stakeholders. It necessitates a willingness to transcend ideological differences, overcome historical grievances, and prioritize the collective well-being of humanity over narrow self-interests. Additionally, it requires leaders to uphold principles of fairness, justice, and equality in their interactions with other nations.

THESIS 53

Our commercial policy should hold an equal and impartial hand,
neither seeking nor granting exclusive favors or preferences.

Throughout history, nations have grappled with the complexities of commercial policy, often oscillating between protectionist measures and free trade principles. The notion of holding an equal and impartial hand in commercial affairs resonates deeply with the fundamental principles of fairness and equity in international trade.

One compelling justification for this approach can be found in the historical example of mercantilism. During the mercantilist era, nations pursued policies aimed at accumulating wealth through exports and accumulating precious metals. However, this often led to conflicts and trade wars as nations sought to secure exclusive trading privileges and monopolies.

In contrast, the principle of impartiality in commercial policy promotes a level playing field for all nations, fostering an environment conducive to peaceful and mutually beneficial trade relations. By avoiding the granting of exclusive favors or preferences, nations can mitigate the risk of provoking trade disputes and retaliatory measures from other countries.

Moreover, history offers numerous examples of the detrimental effects of protectionist policies and trade barriers. The Smoot-Hawley Tariff Act of 1930, for instance, exacerbated the Great Depression by triggering retaliatory tariffs and disrupting global trade flows.

In today's interconnected world, where global supply chains and trade networks are increasingly interdependent, the importance of maintaining an equal and impartial commercial policy cannot be overstated.

Washington's admonition to hold an equal and impartial hand in commercial policy offers valuable guidance for navigating the complexities of international trade. By examining historical examples and contextualizing this principle within broader historical trends, this chapter aims to underscore the importance of promoting fair and equitable trade relations for the benefit of all nations.

THESIS 54

Diffuse and diversify by gentle means the streams of commerce but forcing nothing.

Throughout history, nations that have embraced this principle have often experienced greater economic growth and stability. By fostering an environment of trust and cooperation through trade, countries can create mutually beneficial arrangements that enhance their respective economies and contribute to overall global development.

An example of the successful implementation of this principle can be found in the historical context of the Silk Road. The ancient trade routes that connected civilizations across Asia, Europe, and Africa facilitated the exchange of goods, ideas, and cultures through peaceful commercial interactions. This diffusion of commerce not only stimulated economic growth but also fostered cultural exchange and diplomatic ties between distant lands.

Moreover, Washington's admonition to avoid forcing commerce highlights the importance of respecting the sovereignty and autonomy of other nations. By refraining from imposing trade agreements or policies through coercion, countries can build trust and goodwill with their trading partners, laying the foundation for long-term cooperation and prosperity.

In today's interconnected world, where global trade plays a pivotal role in driving economic growth and development, Washington's advice remains as relevant as ever. By embracing the principle of diffusing and diversifying commerce through peaceful means, nations can navigate complex geopolitical challenges and build resilient economic networks that benefit all stakeholders involved.

THESIS 55

Establish powers so disposed to give trade a stable course, to define the rights of our business owners, and to enable the government to support them under conventional rules of trade.

The establishment of clear and fair trade regulations and the protection of business rights have been essential in fostering an environment conducive to commerce. By providing a framework of stability and predictability, governments can instill confidence among business owners and investors, encouraging them to engage in trade and investment activities.

One notable historical example of the benefits of stable trade relations can be found in the Hanseatic League, a confederation of merchant guilds and market towns in medieval Europe. The Hanseatic League established a network of trade routes and ports across the Baltic and North Seas, facilitating the exchange of goods and fostering economic cooperation among member cities. Through the establishment of common trade regulations and the protection of merchants' rights, the Hanseatic League played a crucial role in promoting commerce and prosperity in the region.

Furthermore, Washington's emphasis on enabling government support under conventional trade rules highlights the importance of aligning trade policies with international norms and standards. By adhering to established trade rules and agreements, governments can minimize trade barriers and promote fair and transparent trade practices. This not only benefits domestic businesses but also fosters cooperation and trust among trading partners on the global stage.

In today's interconnected world, where trade plays a vital role in driving economic growth and development, the principles outlined in Thesis 54 remain as relevant as ever. By establishing powers that are committed to providing a stable trade environment, defining the rights of business owners, and supporting them under conventional trade rules, governments can create a foundation for sustainable economic growth and prosperity.

THESIS 56

It is folly for one nation to look for disinterested favors from another; for that it must pay with a portion of its independence.

The concept of reciprocity, whereby nations seek to advance their interests through mutually beneficial exchanges, has long been a cornerstone of diplomatic relations. However, Washington's warning serves as a reminder that expecting favors without acknowledging the underlying dynamics of power and self-interest can lead to disillusionment and disappointment.

One illustrative historical example of this principle can be found in the relationship between colonial powers and their colonies during the age of imperialism. European powers often extended their influence and control over distant territories under the guise of providing civilizing missions or economic opportunities. However, these ostensibly benevolent gestures were often accompanied by the imposition of colonial rule and the suppression of indigenous rights and freedoms. The colonies, in return for the purported benefits of civilization and development, were required to cede a portion of their independence to their colonial masters.

Furthermore, Washington's warning resonates with the realities of modern geopolitics, where nations engage in strategic alliances and partnerships to advance their interests on the global stage. In an interconnected world characterized by complex power dynamics and competing interests, nations must navigate a delicate balance between pursuing their own interests and accommodating the demands of others. The notion of disinterested favors becomes increasingly untenable as nations seek to assert their sovereignty and autonomy in an ever-changing geopolitical landscape.

Thesis 55 serves as a sobering reminder of the realities of international relations: nations cannot expect to receive favors from others without acknowledging the inherent complexities and trade-offs involved. By understanding the dynamics of power and self-interest, nations can adopt a more pragmatic and realistic approach to diplomacy, one that prioritizes the protection of their own independence while engaging with others in a spirit of mutual respect and cooperation.

THESIS 57

Never avoid opportunities by cultivating peace with all nations, no matter their system of governance.

Nations have always grappled with the intricacies of diplomacy and the pursuit of peaceful coexistence with other states. Washington's admonition to embrace diplomatic opportunities resonates profoundly, highlighting the value of engaging in dialogue and negotiation to address differences and prevent conflicts. By fostering peaceful relations with all nations, states can contribute to global stability and promote mutual understanding.

In today's interconnected world, characterized by diverse political ideologies and competing interests, diplomacy plays a pivotal role in resolving disputes and advancing common goals. The example of successful diplomatic initiatives underscores the importance of Washington's counsel, demonstrating how dialogue and cooperation can lead to meaningful outcomes even in the face of adversity.

Many nations we view as "permanent" adversaries today are often products of short-term strategies and reactions to recent wrongs perpetuated by one side or the other. History has shown that generational change, coupled with peace and trade, can reduce tensions between formerly belligerent nations. Vietnam is a prime example of this reality. By being patient, maintaining a defensive posture, and allowing nations that may seem belligerent today to evolve, we can nurture the notion of liberty that will grow in the hearts of future generations who feel safe and prosperous.

I witnessed this firsthand in the Soviet Union in 1990. I met Russians who were ready for a more open society, and I am convinced that fostering this openness would have led to a more peaceful Russia. However, the expansion of the NATO military pact undermined this opportunity.

As of February 2023, almost 65% of Iran's population was under 35 years old. The restlessness of this younger generation is evident in the recent spate of uprisings that have occurred in Iran over the past decade. These young people are ready for change and we as a nation need to build our policy around the goal of inspiring their sense of freedom rather than being goaded by the hardline element in the current government to react in a way that could alienate the more liberal elements in the country. We must find a balance to contain the aggressive nature of the current government while allowing opportunity to cultivate a positive relationship with a new generation of leaders.

Yet in the war initiated against Iran by the Trump administration on February 28, 2026, we risked abandoning this opportunity altogether. By defaulting to force over engagement, we may be reinforcing the very hardline elements we seek to contain, while closing the door on a generation that has already shown a willingness to move toward greater openness. What could have been a moment to cultivate long-term change may instead become another chapter in a cycle of hostility that delays it for decades.

THESIS 58

By interweaving our destiny with that of any part of Europe, Africa, Asia, or the Middle East, we entangle our peace and prosperity in the toils of localized ambition or rivalry.

Washington's admonition in his original address was focused on the world he knew, with European powers being the most disruptive, but it is appropriate to include the expanded global nature of our challenges with the inclusion of the Middle East, Africa, and Asia, for it still serves as a prescient reminder of the dangers inherent in becoming embroiled in conflicts or rivalries beyond one's borders. By interweaving our destiny with those of distant regions, we risk jeopardizing their own peace and prosperity.

An example from history that underscores the wisdom of Washington's advice is the entanglement of European powers in the affairs of the Middle East during the 19th century. In their pursuit of imperial ambitions and strategic interests, European nations became embroiled in conflicts and rivalries that ultimately undermined their own stability and prosperity. The consequences of this entanglement reverberated for generations, leading to enduring tensions and conflicts in the region.

Similarly, the entanglement of great powers in the affairs of Africa and Asia during the era of colonial expansion illustrates the perils of extending influence beyond one's borders. Nations that sought to exert control over distant territories often found themselves drawn into protracted conflicts and costly endeavors that strained their resources and undermined their domestic stability.

To be candid, it is unrealistic to assume that a relatively young nation like the United States, with a population that often lacks a deep understanding of the complex histories of other countries and their peoples, can effectively mitigate the localized rivalries and social tensions that have persisted for millennia.

THESIS 59

It is our true policy to steer clear of permanent alliances with any portion of the foreign world.

The United States, in particular, has faced numerous temptations to form permanent alliances with other countries, especially during times of conflict and upheaval. However, Washington's counsel reminds us of the dangers inherent in such commitments and the importance of maintaining sovereign independence.

One notable example from history is the United States' decision to avoid entanglement in the affairs of Europe during the Napoleonic Wars. While

European powers were embroiled in a struggle for dominance, the United States remained neutral, preserving its autonomy, and avoiding the potentially devastating consequences of alignment with one side or the other.

There is a school of thought among some that believes the breaking of this precedent and actively siding with combatants in World War I so upset the traditional balance of powers in Europe that the one-sided outcome of that war led to the inevitability of the reactionary rise of fascism in the defeated nations and an even more devastating conflict.

THESIS 60

We should not leave our own land to stand upon foreign ground.

This thesis is one that does not originate from Washington's farewell address but comes from my own perspective that is rooted in the American constitutional tradition of avoiding a permanent standing army, rooted in the founders' mistrust of large military forces due to their potential for corruption and tyranny. This principle is compromised when the United States establishes and maintains standing armies in other nations. The presence of these forces can foster dependency, create local resentment, and entangle the U.S. in foreign conflicts, undermining its commitment to a limited and controlled military establishment. Additionally, the corruptive influences that the founders feared domestically are merely transplanted abroad, perpetuating cycles of instability and erosion of the host nation's sovereignty, which ultimately conflicts with the foundational values of American constitutionalism.

———◆———

Part IV

HOW SHOULD WE ENSURE THESE FOREIGN MISCHIEFS ARE MINIMIZED?

The strong do what they can, and the weak suffer what they must. To be powerful, one must be willing to wield that power with justice and integrity.

—THUCYDIDES

THESIS 61

The president cannot send military troops into harm's way inside the domain of a foreign nation without a formal declaration of war by Congress.

This thesis underscores a fundamental principle enshrined in the United States Constitution—the separation of powers between the executive and legislative branches when it comes to matters of war and peace. Upholding this principle is crucial to preserving the system of checks and balances that safeguard against the concentration of power and the reckless pursuit of military conflicts.

Throughout history, the unchecked power of a single ruler to wage war has often led to disastrous consequences. The Founding Fathers, drawing upon the lessons of the past, sought to establish a system that would prevent such calamities. The requirement for a formal declaration of war by Congress serves as a crucial safeguard, preventing the president from unilaterally committing the nation's resources and lives of its citizens to military conflicts.

The origins of this principle can be traced back to the English Bill of Rights of 1689, which established the supremacy of Parliament over the monarch in matters of war and peace. This concept was further reinforced by the experiences of the American colonists during the Revolutionary War, where they witnessed firsthand the perils of unchecked executive power.

In the aftermath of the war, the Framers of the Constitution recognized the need to distribute the war powers between the executive and legislative branches. The president, as commander-in-chief, would have the authority to direct the military once a conflict had been initiated, but the decision to engage in war itself would rest with Congress.

Article I, Section 8 of the Constitution grants Congress the power "To declare War, grant Letters of Marque and Reprisal, and make Rules concerning Captures on Land and Water." This provision ensures that the decision to commit the nation to war is not made by a single individual but rather through a deliberative process involving the representatives of the people.

The requirement for a formal declaration of war serves as a crucial check on the executive branch, forcing the president to make a compelling case for military action and ensuring that such a momentous decision is not taken lightly. It also provides a clear legal basis for the use of force, ensuring that the nation's military actions are grounded in the rule of law.

Throughout American history, there have been instances where presidents have sought to circumvent the constitutional requirement for a formal declaration of war. The United States has gone to war without a formalized declaration 125 times and only 11 with formal declarations. We have been in a state of war for 20 of the past 25 years. It is self-evident that we must address this issue directly and head-on before the next conflict is justified by the executive branch.

THESIS 62

The USA is to honor all obligations that have been signed, but to seek in all future relations a status of neutrality.

The principle of neutrality is a delicate balance that has profound implications for a nation's foreign policy and its standing on the global stage. This approach, rooted in the desire to avoid entangling alliances and maintain an independent course, has been a recurring theme throughout American history, with both successes and challenges.

The origins of this principle can be traced back to the Founding Fathers, who were deeply influenced by the experiences of the American Revolution and the desire to chart an independent path for the fledgling nation.

This vision was rooted in the belief that entangling alliances could embroil the United States in conflicts that were not in its national interest and could compromise its hard-won independence. The founders sought to establish a nation that would be a beacon of liberty, free from the complex web of European alliances and rivalries that had plagued the continent for centuries. Today, we see the same entangling alliances and rivalries plaguing the Middle East.

While the pursuit of neutrality was a guiding principle, Washington also recognized the importance of honoring existing obligations and treaties. The United States, as a newly established nation, understood the need to cultivate a reputation for reliability and trustworthiness on the international stage. Failure to uphold its commitments would undermine its credibility and standing among the community of nations.

This principle was put to the test during the Quasi-War with France in the late 1790s, when the United States found itself embroiled in an undeclared naval conflict with its former Revolutionary ally. Despite the tensions, the Adams administration remained committed to upholding the existing treaties and obligations with France, while simultaneously asserting its neutrality and avoiding a full-scale war.

The United States has grappled with the challenges of maintaining neutrality while upholding its obligations and protecting its national interests. The policy of neutrality was tested during the World Wars, when the United States initially sought to remain neutral but ultimately found itself drawn into the conflicts due to the threat posed by the Axis powers and the need to defend its allies and interests.

In the post-World War II era, the United States embraced a more active role on the global stage, forming alliances and taking on leadership responsibilities within the international community, leading us down a dark path of alliances that could easily entangle us in another unintended war.

The pursuit of neutrality while honoring existing obligations is a delicate balance that requires careful navigation and a clear understanding of a nation's priorities and interests. While the challenges of maintaining neutrality in an increasingly interconnected world are formidable, the commitment to upholding obligations and charting an independent course should be a cornerstone of the United States' approach to international relations.

THESIS 63

Initiate plans to phase out the presence of a standing army in foreign lands.

In terms of overseas deployments, there were over 228,390 U.S. military personnel stationed in foreign countries as of September 2023, 168,571 of which were active-duty troops.

The perils of prolonged military occupation and the presence of a standing army in foreign lands have been well-documented throughout history. From the Roman Empire's struggles to maintain control over its vast territories to the challenges faced by modern superpowers in their interventions abroad, the costs and consequences of such endeavors have often proven to be substantial.

This idea reflects the American constitutional tradition of avoiding a permanent standing army, rooted in the founders' mistrust of large military forces due to their potential for corruption and tyranny. This principle is compromised when the United States establishes and maintains standing armies in other nations. The presence of these forces can foster dependency, create local resentment, and entangle the U.S. in foreign conflicts, undermining its commitment to a limited and controlled military establishment. Additionally, the corruptive influences that the founders feared domestically are merely transplanted abroad, perpetuating cycles of instability and erosion of the host nation's sovereignty, which ultimately conflicts with the foundational values of American constitutionalism.

The military-industrial complex is emboldened by the U.S. maintaining a large standing army in other nations in several ways:

The need to support and supply a large standing army abroad necessitates significant defense spending. This leads to lucrative contracts for defense contractors, thereby fueling the growth and influence of the military-industrial complex.

A permanent military presence overseas creates a continuous demand for a wide range of military goods and services, from advanced weaponry to logistical support. This sustained demand benefits defense companies and contractors, encouraging further investment in military infrastructure and technology.

The financial interests of the military-industrial complex often translate into political influence. Companies within this complex lobby for policies that support maintaining and expanding military operations abroad, ensuring a steady stream of government contracts and funding.

The presence of U.S. troops in foreign nations provides a justification for the continued expansion of military capabilities and infrastructure. This, in turn, leads to increased budgets and further entrenchment of the military-industrial complex within the national economy and political system.

Keeping a large standing army in other countries normalizes military engagement and intervention as standard practice. This normalization supports the narrative that a strong, pervasive military presence is essential for national security, thereby reinforcing the role and power of the military-industrial complex.

Regions and communities that benefit economically from military bases and related industries become advocates for maintaining these presences. This creates a cycle where local economies become dependent on military spending, further entrenching the military-industrial complex.

In summary, the maintenance of a large standing army in other nations provides the military-industrial complex with financial incentives, political influence, and a continual justification for expansion, thereby reinforcing its power and entrenchment in U.S. policy and society.

THESIS 64

Military training at 18 years of age for qualified men and women to be available for state/home guard active service for a minimum of two years and never to be utilized outside the state of residency unless by order of the governor or a constitutional declaration of war.

The principle of implementing military training for qualified young men and women at the age of 18 is rooted in fostering civic responsibility and preparedness among the nation's youth. This idea has historical roots in American traditions, where a well-trained and disciplined citizenry is viewed as essential for preserving liberty and national defense.

The origins of this principle can be traced back to the earliest days of the American republic. The Founding Fathers, aware of the dangers of standing armies and valuing an armed citizenry, enshrined the concept of a well-regulated militia in the Second Amendment of the Constitution. This tradition of the citizen-soldier was crucial during the Revolutionary War, where ordinary citizens took up arms to defend their fledgling nation against British forces. The resilience and determination of these citizen-soldiers, who embodied civic duty and sacrifice, were pivotal to the success of the American Revolution and laid the groundwork for a legacy that continues to influence military preparedness and national security.

Military training at 18 serves multiple purposes beyond combat readiness. It instills discipline, teamwork, and physical fitness, equipping young people with valuable skills applicable in various aspects of life. This training fosters patriotism and an understanding of the sacrifices needed to safeguard the nation's freedoms. By participating in this program, young citizens gain a profound appreciation for the principles upon which the nation was founded and the responsibilities that come with citizenship. They learn to embrace values of duty, honor, and service, essential for maintaining a free and democratic society.

Moreover, military training at this age ensures the nation has a pool of trained individuals ready for times of crisis or conflict. This preparedness enhances national security and serves as a deterrent against potential adversaries, reinforcing the nation's commitment to self-defense.

However, implementing military training in the modern era must adapt to changing societal norms and evolving security challenges. The integration of advanced technologies and the ethical and moral implications of such training must be carefully considered. The program should instill respect for human rights, the rule of law, and the principles of just warfare, balancing preparedness with ethical conduct.

Additionally, the principle of state/home guard active service complements this by emphasizing state autonomy and local preparedness. Historically, state militias and home guard units have defended local communities and responded to emergencies. Maintaining a well-trained force within each state ensures that states can safeguard their citizens and uphold the rule of law without relying solely on federal intervention. This approach recognizes unique state challenges and empowers local authorities to take decisive action when necessary.

However, the misuse of the National Guard for extended deployments in conflicts such as the Iraq War highlights significant issues with federalism and the constitutional rule of law. The National Guard, intended primarily for domestic emergencies and state defense, was increasingly deployed overseas, straining local resources and disrupting the balance of state and federal responsibilities. This practice not only compromised the original purpose of the National Guard but also undermined the federalist structure by encroaching on states' rights to manage their own military resources. Such actions weaken the foundational principle of state sovereignty, creating a problematic precedent where federal needs override state autonomy, ultimately jeopardizing the effectiveness and readiness of state-level responses to local emergencies.

State/home guard service also promotes civic engagement and team building among citizens. By requiring young people to serve in a state guard, they participate in a common experience that transcends socioeconomic, racial, and cultural differences. This shared service builds bonds among individuals, fostering unity and teamwork. It instills civic duty and responsibility, enhancing commitment to civic values and public service. Participants develop a deeper connection to their local communities, working on projects that directly benefit their neighbors. The service provides opportunities to develop leadership and teamwork skills, encouraging collaboration and mutual support.

In conclusion, the commitment to fostering a well-trained and responsible citizenry through military training and state/home guard service remains a cornerstone of national security and the preservation of liberty. This principle has withstood the test of time and continues to guide efforts to cultivate a generation of dedicated and capable citizens, ready to answer the call of duty when needed. The misuse of the National Guard for overseas deployments must be addressed to preserve the constitutional balance of power and maintain the integrity of federalism.

THESIS 65

Our nation's foreign policy initiatives must never be determined by profit-driven corporations.

Throughout history, the pursuit of profit by powerful corporations has often intersected with the realm of foreign policy, sometimes with disastrous consequences. The legacy of colonialism and the exploitation of natural resources in developing nations by multinational corporations serve as stark reminders of the perils of allowing private interests to dictate the course of international relations. One of the most notorious examples is the United Fruit Company's involvement in the overthrow of the democratically elected government of Guatemala in 1954. The company's vast banana plantations and economic interests in the region were threatened by the Guatemalan government's land reform policies, prompting the company to lobby the U.S. government for intervention. The subsequent CIA-backed coup not only undermined Guatemalan sovereignty but also sowed the seeds of decades of civil unrest and instability in the region. There is an unfortunate thread of connectivity to our nation's interventionism 70 years ago and the immigrant crisis today.

Foreign policy decisions, which have far-reaching implications for a nation's security, economic well-being, and global standing, must be guided by the collective interests of the people and the principles enshrined in the nation's constitution. By insulating foreign policy from the influence of corporate interests, the nation upholds its commitment to self-determination and the pursuit of policies that serve the greater good. This principle recognizes that the pursuit of profit, while a legitimate endeavor in the realm of business, must never supersede the broader national interests or undermine the democratic processes that shape a nation's international relations.

Ensuring that foreign policy initiatives are not determined by profit-driven corporations also promotes transparency and accountability in the realm of international affairs. When corporate interests are allowed to influence foreign policy decisions, there is a risk of obscuring the true motivations behind such initiatives and undermining public trust in the government's actions. By maintaining a clear separation between corporate interests and foreign policy formulation, the nation can foster an environment of openness and public scrutiny, where the rationale behind diplomatic and military initiatives can be openly debated and scrutinized. This transparency not only strengthens the democratic process but also enhances the nation's credibility on the global stage, reinforcing its commitment to principled and ethical conduct in international relations.

What are the policy initiatives that will help encourage a separation between corporate needs and that of the U.S. government? Reducing the ability of corporate money and individual wealth to influence political leadership; those remedies can be found most prominently in the theses listed in chapters II and VIII.

Part V

WASHINGTON'S CONCERNS ABOUT FISCAL RESPONSIBILITY

The borrower is servant to the lender.

—**PROVERBS 22:7 (KING JAMES BIBLE)**

THESIS 66

As a very important source of strength and security, we must protect our public credit.

THESIS 67

Preserve public credit by using it as sparingly as possible.

One of the most notable examples of the importance of public credit can be found in the efforts of Alexander Hamilton, the first secretary of the Treasury of the United States. In his seminal 1789 report, Hamilton emphasized the vital role of supporting public credit, stating that it was essential "to furnish new resources both to agriculture and commerce" and to establish the young nation's financial independence and credibility on the global stage.

The protection of public credit has been a cornerstone of national security throughout history, as it has provided our government with the means to finance military efforts, respond to emergencies, and safeguard our sovereignty. During times of war or crisis, a strong public credit has allowed the U.S. to raise funds swiftly, ensuring that we have the resources necessary to defend our interests and protect our citizens.

Our own American Revolution was financed through a combination of domestic borrowing and substantial foreign loans, primarily from France, Spain, and the Netherlands. This borrowing was crucial to the success of the American war effort, allowing the Continental Army to be supplied, paid, and supported in critical battles. The repayment of these debts and the establishment of a sound financial system were vital steps in the early years of the United States, helping to secure its economic future and independence.

Beyond its practical applications, the protection of public credit has also been a powerful symbol of a nation's strength and credibility. Governments that have consistently honored their debt obligations and maintained a strong public credit have garnered the respect and confidence of their citizens and the international community alike.

This confidence has been a source of stability, attracting foreign investment and fostering an environment conducive to economic growth and prosperity. Conversely, nations that have failed to protect their public credit have often found themselves mired in economic turmoil, facing diminished credibility and limited access to the resources necessary for their development and security.

Unfortunately, we have failed miserably in protecting public credit. Our elected representatives have turned into salespeople trying to deliver funding to pet projects in their districts, thus empowering themselves at the expense of public credit.

The U.S. federal government has a statutory debt limit, a cap set by Congress on the amount of debt the government is authorized to borrow to meet its existing legal obligations. When this limit is reached, Congress must pass legislation to increase it. This process has become a routine yet contentious aspect of fiscal policy, often leading to political brinkmanship and uncertainty.

Raising the debt limit is necessary to prevent the U.S. from defaulting on its obligations, which would have catastrophic economic consequences. However, the frequent need to raise the limit highlights the inefficiency of the current system. Instead of addressing the underlying issues of fiscal imbalance and unsustainable spending, the debt limit is repeatedly increased, allowing the government to continue borrowing without implementing meaningful reforms.

Only Denmark operates under a system like the U.S. debt ceiling. The few countries that do have a debt ceiling have it tied to GDP instead of a fixed amount. However, most countries manage their public finances through annual budgets and medium- to long-term fiscal frameworks, which do not require periodic legislative approval to increase borrowing limits. These systems are often more efficient and less prone to political deadlock, as they provide a structured approach to managing public debt within predefined fiscal rules.

The process of repeatedly increasing the debt limit to maintain public credit is inefficient for several reasons:

Each time the debt ceiling is approached, it creates a period of political uncertainty and potential economic instability. This uncertainty can negatively impact financial markets and erode investor confidence.

Raising the debt limit without addressing the root causes of fiscal imbalance merely postpones necessary reforms. It perpetuates a cycle of borrowing and spending that is unsustainable in the long term.

The political standoffs that often accompany debt ceiling debates increase the risk of a default, which would have severe repercussions for the global economy and America's creditworthiness.

The repeated crises and debates over the debt ceiling can undermine public trust in the government's ability to manage its finances responsibly.

THESIS 68

*Avoid the accumulation of debt, not only by shunning occasions of
expense, but by vigorous exertion in time of peace to discharge the debts.*

THESIS 69

*We must not throw upon posterity the burden which we ourselves
ought to bear.*

In recent decades, the national debt of the United States has soared to
unprecedented levels, underscoring the urgency and wisdom of Washington's
admonition. This quote speaks to the responsibility of the current generation
to manage fiscal policy prudently and avoid passing an unsustainable financial
burden onto future generations.

Over the past 30 years, the U.S. national debt has escalated dramatically.
In 1990, the national debt was approximately $3.2 trillion. As of spring 2024,
the national debt has ballooned to over $32 trillion, representing a tenfold
increase. This alarming growth rate highlights a trend of fiscal irresponsibility,
characterized by persistent budget deficits and the compounding nature of
interest payments on the debt.

The current debt situation is comparable to the debt levels incurred during
World War II, a period of extraordinary national expenditure necessitated by
global conflict. At the end of World War II, the U.S. debt-to-GDP ratio peaked
at about 119%, driven by the immense costs of wartime spending. However,
this debt was managed and reduced significantly in the subsequent decades
through a combination of strong economic growth and fiscal discipline. In
contrast, the current debt-to-GDP ratio has once again approached and
surpassed these historical levels, but without the same immediate and clear
existential justification. The current high debt is more the result of prolonged
fiscal imbalances and policy choices rather than an unavoidable emergency.

Kicking the can down the road by deferring debt reduction measures to future administrations and generations is not just imprudent but deeply irresponsible. This approach disregards the economic principle of sustainable fiscal policy and ignores the adverse long-term effects of high debt levels. Persistent high debt undermines economic stability, increases borrowing costs, and limits the government's ability to respond to future crises.

At current revenue levels, paying off the national debt is a daunting challenge. In 2023, the federal government collected approximately $4.9 trillion in total revenues. However, with annual expenditures consistently outpacing revenues, the federal government continues to run significant budget deficits. For instance, the budget deficit for 2023 was around $1.5 trillion. Assuming no growth in debt and directing all revenues solely to debt repayment (which is impractical as it ignores necessary government spending), it would take over six years just to pay off the principal amount of the current debt, not accounting for accruing interest.

In reality, the scenario is even grimmer due to the need for continued public spending on essential services, defense, and other obligations. Consequently, the timeline for substantial debt reduction extends well beyond the foreseeable future under the current fiscal trajectory.

The burgeoning national debt imposes a significant burden on other critical needs. Interest payments on the debt are consuming an ever larger share of the federal budget. In fiscal year 2023, interest payments alone amounted to approximately $475 billion. This amount is projected to increase as interest rates rise and the debt grows, crowding out funding for vital programs such as infrastructure, education, health care, and social services.

Moreover, the federal debt and the associated tax burden make it increasingly difficult for states to raise the revenue needed for local services. As the federal government allocates more resources to service its debt, less funding is available for the foundational requirements of a functioning government. By failing to address the growing national debt, we risk imposing an untenable financial burden on posterity, compromising their economic stability and limiting their ability to invest in future prosperity. It is imperative that we adopt sustainable fiscal policies that balance the budget, reduce deficits, and prioritize debt reduction. This requires difficult but necessary decisions about spending and revenue generation to ensure that we do not shirk our responsibilities, leaving an insurmountable debt for future generations to bear. The time for action is now, for the longer we delay, the heavier the burden will become.

THESIS 70

It is essential that we should practically bear in mind that toward the payment of debts there must be revenue.

THESIS 71

To have revenue there must be taxes; no taxes can be devised which are not more or less inconvenient and unpleasant.

Theses 70 and 71 together highlight the critical role of taxation in maintaining the financial health of a nation. Revenue approved by elected representatives ensures that the taxation system reflects the will of the people, legitimizing it as a constitutional and democratic process rather than an act of theft. Taxation, when conducted through constitutional means, is a direct expression of the collective decision-making of the electorate, represented by their chosen officials and should not be referred to as being "stolen," implying ultralegal measures are at play and thus undermining the notion that is a necessary component of responsible governance. Additionally, while it's important to "wish" that government should act more like a business, we must remember that businesses are primarily designed to generate a profit from the revenue they collect, whereas government operates to serve the public interest, which includes funding essential services through taxation.

Emphasizing this distinction ensures that the necessary revenues are raised to meet public obligations and pay off national debts, ultimately fostering a stable and accountable governance structure.

THESIS 72

Hold the maxim no less applicable to the public than to private affairs, that honesty is always the best policy.

Being honest with the American public about national debts and the allocation of tax revenues is essential for maintaining the trust of citizens who bear the financial burden of government services and goods. Transparency in fiscal matters ensures that taxpayers understand how their money is being spent and fosters a sense of accountability among elected representatives. This transparency not only legitimizes the government's fiscal policies but also encourages a more informed and engaged electorate, ultimately strengthening the democratic process.

———— ❖ ————

Part VI

HOW SHOULD WE MAINTAIN FISCAL RESPONSIBILITY?

Do your duty and a little more, and the future will take care of itself.
—ANDREW CARNEGIE

IN THE ANNALS OF AMERICAN history, few challenges have loomed as large as the nation's current debt crisis. As of 2024, the national debt soars to an unprecedented 128.1% of the country's annual economic output, surpassing even the staggering levels witnessed in the aftermath of World War II; the United States finds itself treading a perilous path, one that threatens to undermine its economic stability, national security, and global standing.

This unprecedented level of debt, breaking records during peacetime, starkly contrasts with the nation's long-standing tradition of fiscal discipline and prudence. It serves as a somber reminder of the repercussions of unchecked spending, misguided tax policies, and the economic fallout from unforeseen crises, such as the COVID-19 pandemic.

Yet, even in the face of this daunting challenge, the nation can find solace in its rich history of overcoming fiscal adversity. From the Revolutionary War to the Civil War, and from the Great Depression to the two World Wars, the United States has consistently demonstrated its ability to navigate turbulent economic waters and steer toward prosperity.

It is this legacy of perseverance and fiscal responsibility that must serve as a guiding light as the nation confronts the current debt crisis. The lessons of the past, embodied in the visionary leadership of figures like Alexander Hamilton and the steadfast commitment to debt reduction following World War II, offer hope and inspiration.

The debt crisis is not merely a financial obstacle; it is a trial of the nation's determination, a crucible in which enduring principles of fiscal prudence, intergenerational equity, and the pursuit of the common good will be reaffirmed. It calls upon all Americans to embrace the hard-earned lessons of the past and to chart a courageous course toward a future where the blessings of liberty and prosperity are preserved for generations to come.

It is painfully evident the national government has lost the discipline necessary to manage the funds it automatically collects from our paychecks. A radical change is needed to ensure we are not permanently and irreparably damaged by our current and ever-growing debt burden. Though I believe the implementation of most of the 40 policy points within the 95 Theses will help encourage a more disciplined approach that our nation used to have, the debt burden requires a revolutionary approach.

As we navigate this challenging path, we must remain engaged in extraordinary actions for this issue and be unwavering in our commitment to the ideals that have guided the nation through its darkest hours in the past.

As it is during times of adversity that the true character of a person is revealed, so it is true for the nation as well.

THESIS 73

Create a time-definable plan to pay off the majority percentage of the debt of the federal government.

THESIS 74

Utilize a progressive income tax on corporate profits and/or capital gains if other modes of taxation, federal spending cuts, economic growth, and the liquidation of underutilized federal property do not meet established goals.

THESIS 75

Any additional revenue outlined in Thesis 74 must be utilized to lower the debt to the goals established within a time frame most conducive to striking an acceptable balance between growth and debt reduction.

In the annals of economic stewardship, one principle stands paramount: the imperative of responsible debt management. From the corridors of history to the arenas of contemporary policymaking, the specter of debt has loomed large, challenging leaders to chart a course toward fiscal sustainability. At the heart of this endeavor lies a pivotal insight, as articulated by George Washington, that resonates across epochs and administrations: "It is essential that we should practically bear in mind that toward the payment of debts there must be revenue."

The profound significance of Washington's observation, tracing its echoes through time and illuminating its relevance in shaping prudent fiscal policies, cannot be overstated. The recognition that debt repayment hinges on the availability of revenue has served as a lodestar for leaders navigating the treacherous waters of fiscal management. In past centuries, nations have grappled with the difficult task of repaying debt while safeguarding their citizens' welfare. In moments of crisis and tranquility alike, the quest for economic equilibrium has demanded innovative strategies and unwavering resolve.

Against this backdrop, the proposal outlined in Thesis 74 emerges by advocating for a time-definable plan to address the federal government's debt burden. The thesis seeks to marry historical wisdom with contemporary exigencies. Central to this plan is the notion of creating a short-term increased progressive income tax on upper incomes, contingent upon federal spending cuts and other creative revenue streams fail to meet established goals. This approach highlights how debt repayment strategies can evolve by incorporating past endeavors into current ones, updating them to reflect modern challenges.

A strategy deserving serious consideration is the sale of underutilized federal real estate. The federal government owns approximately 640 million acres, or 28% of the United States' land area. Excluding the 84 million acres of national parks, which should remain protected, this leaves 556 million acres for potential discussion. Decisions regarding these properties should involve local communities most affected by them.

For instance, in South Carolina, the federal government controls nearly 600,000 acres in the National Forest program, land acquired during the Great Depression to address sub-marginal farmland, soil erosion, stream flow regulation, and timber growth. However, these areas have since experienced economic depression due to a lack of property tax revenue and the creation of "islands" of population surrounded by mostly uninhabited land.

Selling a portion of these assets, while preserving essential watersheds and wildlife corridors, could stimulate economic growth in isolated communities like Whitmire and McCormick. The land sale could be targeted to those who can create income as independent farmers and develop a more sustainable local food supply.

There are many ways this could be achieved and benefit more than just debt reduction, but we must get serious with the problem and start developing workable goals for the surrounding communities that would benefit from this program.

THESIS 76

*Amend the 16th Amendment to create a federal income tax only
to fund the investment necessitated by a formal declaration of war
by Congress.*

In the history of fiscal policy, few measures have had as profound an impact as the enactment of the 16th Amendment, which established the federal income tax system in the United States. However, the implementation of this amendment has encountered notable hurdles over time, leading to questions about its effectiveness and suitability.

The justification for this proposed reform lies in the lessons of history. Throughout the centuries, nations have grappled with the challenge of funding wars, often resorting to taxation as a means of generating the necessary revenue. From ancient civilizations to modern superpowers, the financing of wars has been a constant preoccupation of governments, shaping the course of history and the fate of nations.

In the context of the United States, the 16th Amendment represented a watershed moment in fiscal policy, granting the federal government broad powers to levy income taxes on its citizens. While initially intended as a means of funding government operations, the amendment has been criticized for enabling excessive government spending and expanding the scope of federal authority beyond its intended limits.

Moreover, the income tax system has become corrupted over time, with the primary method of collecting revenue involving the confiscation of a portion of wages from the working class. Meanwhile, many corporations exploit tax deductions that have been engineered to benefit the more privileged class of citizens. This disparity highlights the inequities inherent in the current system, where the burden of taxation disproportionately affects ordinary workers while allowing wealthier entities to minimize their tax liabilities.

Additionally, when the government confiscates this money and it is later shown that too much was paid, the refund does not include interest on the government's use of that money. This practice further underscores the imbalance and unfairness in the system, as taxpayers effectively provide the government with an interest-free loan.

The proposal outlined in Thesis 76 seeks to address these concerns by narrowing the scope of the federal income tax to fund investments necessitated by a formal declaration of war by the House of Representatives. This approach reflects a fundamental principle of fiscal prudence: that taxes should be levied for specific, clearly defined purposes, rather than for general government spending.

By limiting the federal income tax to war funding, policymakers can ensure greater transparency and accountability in the use of taxpayer dollars while also encouraging a more measured approach to military intervention. History has shown that wars waged without adequate funding mechanisms can lead to unsustainable debt burdens, economic instability, and social upheaval. By tying taxation directly to the costs of war, this reform would, most importantly, mitigate these risks of short-term reactionary response to challenges overseas and promote a more responsible approach to national defense.

This reform reflects a commitment to fiscal prudence, transparency, and accountability, drawing on the lessons of history to shape a more sustainable path forward for the United States.

THESIS 77

Any federal income tax created for a specific war debt expires once those war debts are paid for.

The imposition of federal income taxes has long been a contentious issue in the United States, with debates raging over the scope, duration, and purpose of such levies. One particularly contentious aspect of income taxation is its use to finance war debts, a practice that has significant implications for fiscal policy and government accountability. Implementing a sunset provision for federal income taxes created for specific war debts is important, as historical examples illustrate the need for fiscal responsibility and transparency in wartime financing.

Over time, countries have utilized taxation to finance wars and similar military engagements. Nonetheless, persisting with wartime taxes well beyond the end of conflicts can adversely impact both the economy and society. Introducing a sunset clause for income taxes related to war can guarantee fair distribution of the wartime financial load and prevent taxpayers from being excessively encumbered by levies tied to historical conflicts.

The history of income taxation in the United States is replete with examples of wartime tax measures and their aftermath. During periods of conflict such as World War I, World War II, and the Vietnam War, the federal government implemented income taxes to finance the enormous costs of war. While these taxes were initially justified as temporary measures to meet the exigencies of wartime, many of them persisted long after the wars themselves had ended.

One of the most notable examples of prolonged wartime taxation is the Revenue Act of 1942, which introduced the Victory Tax—a temporary tax levied to finance World War II. Despite its purported temporary nature, the Victory Tax remained in effect for several years after the war ended, leading to widespread public dissatisfaction and calls for reform.

The implementation of a sunset provision for federal income taxes created for specific war debts would require legislative action by the U.S. Congress. The provision could be included as part of broader tax reform legislation or as a stand-alone measure aimed at promoting fiscal responsibility and accountability in wartime financing.

By ensuring that such taxes expire once the associated debts are paid off, policymakers can promote fiscal responsibility, transparency, and accountability in wartime financing.

THESIS 78

The tax burden on citizens to finance services legislated by their elected representatives should come primarily from state governments.

The distribution of tax responsibilities to fund governmental services has remained a topic of debate and dispute within the United States for an extended period. At the heart of this discussion lies the inquiry into which governmental level—be it federal, state, or local—ought to shoulder the primary duty for taxation and revenue generation. State governments should bear the primary burden of funding legislated public services, drawing on historical precedent to demonstrate the benefits of decentralized taxation.

Thesis 78 is grounded in the principles of federalism and subsidiarity, which endorse decentralization of powers and duties to the most feasible local level of governance. By granting state governments increased fiscal independence and revenue-raising capabilities, policymakers can enhance local accountability, responsiveness, and effectiveness in delivering public services.

In the early years of the republic, state governments played a dominant role in taxation, relying primarily on property taxes, sales taxes, and excise taxes to fund their operations. There has been a dynamic interplay between the federal, state, and local governments when it comes to taxation in the United States. However, the growth of the federal government in the 20th century brought about a significant shift in the balance of taxation, with the federal government assuming a larger share of the tax burden through the imposition of income taxes and other levies.

One of the most significant developments in federal-state fiscal relations was the passage of the 16th Amendment in 1913, which authorized Congress to levy income taxes directly from citizens. This amendment marked a departure from the traditional reliance on indirect taxes and greatly expanded the federal government's revenue-raising powers. Subsequent decades saw the federal government increasingly assert its authority in taxation, often at the expense of state and local governments.

Thesis 78 advocates for a rebalancing of fiscal responsibilities between the federal government and state governments, with a greater emphasis on state-level taxation for funding legislated services. This approach offers several benefits, including:

- Enhanced Accountability: By financing services through state-level taxation, citizens can hold their state elected representatives directly accountable for the allocation of resources and the delivery of services. This localized accountability fosters greater transparency and responsiveness in governance.

- Fiscal Flexibility: State governments are better positioned to tailor tax policies to the unique needs and preferences of their residents. This flexibility enables states to experiment with different revenue sources and tax structures to promote economic growth and social welfare.

- Efficient Resource Allocation: Decentralized taxation allows states to allocate resources more efficiently, directing funding to areas of greatest need and priority. This targeted approach to resource allocation enhances the effectiveness and efficiency of government services like mental health intervention and K-12 education.

Thesis 78 proposes a redistribution of the tax burden, emphasizing that state governments should bear the primary responsibility for financing legislated services. Informed by historical examples and federalist principles, this recommendation aims to bolster local accountability, fiscal adaptability, and optimal resource distribution. By granting state governments increased fiscal independence, policymakers can improve the responsiveness, efficiency, and long-term viability of government services to the advantage of the entire citizenry.

THESIS 79

Federal taxes should be based primarily on consumption of goods:
local, interstate, imports.

Within discussions about taxation in the United States, the manner in which federal taxes are imposed has been a continual point of contention. Thesis 79 contends that federal taxes should predominantly hinge on the consumption of goods, whether they're domestic, interstate, or imports. This stance is supported by historical illustrations, emphasizing its effectiveness in fostering economic growth, equity, and fiscal endurance.

Federal taxes should be predominantly derived from the consumption of goods rather than other forms of taxation such as income or wealth. This approach is rooted in the principle of broad-based taxation, which spreads the tax burden across a wide range of economic activities and ensures that all individuals contribute to the funding of government services. Moreover, by focusing on consumption-based taxes, policymakers can avoid the economic distortions and compliance costs associated with other forms of taxation.

The concept of consumption-based taxation has deep roots in American history, dating back to the earliest days of the republic. In the 18th and 19th centuries, the federal government relied primarily on tariffs and excise taxes on goods such as alcohol, tobacco, and luxury items to fund its operations. These taxes were relatively simple to administer and enforce, making them an attractive source of revenue for the young nation. One of the most significant developments in the history of consumption-based taxation was the passage of the Tariff Act of 1789, which imposed duties on imported goods entering the United States. This legislation not only provided much-needed revenue for the federal government but also served to protect domestic industries from foreign competition, laying the groundwork for economic growth and industrial development.

Thesis 79 proposes a reversion to the fundamentals of consumption-based taxation to finance the federal government. Through imposing taxes on goods consumption, policymakers aim to establish a fair and transparent tax system, where individuals contribute based on their consumption capacity rather than their income or wealth. Additionally, this strategy holds promise in stimulating economic activity by encouraging saving and investment while discouraging overconsumption. Moreover, consumption-based taxes are less susceptible to evasion and avoidance than other forms of taxation, as they are tied directly to economic transactions rather than subjective measures of income or wealth. This enhances the efficiency and effectiveness of tax collection, reducing the burden on both taxpayers and government agencies.

THESIS 80

States should have the exclusive right to create a permanent income tax
as well as sales tax.

This proposition is grounded in the principles of federalism, which prioritize decentralized governance and recognize the diverse needs and preferences of individual states and localities. The issue of state taxation autonomy has been a source of debate and disagreement. During the early years of the republic, states predominantly relied on property taxes and tariffs to finance their operations, with minimal interference from the federal government. However, this dynamic shifted with the adoption of the 16th Amendment to the U.S. Constitution in 1913, which granted the federal government the authority to impose income taxes.

While the 16th Amendment bolstered the federal government's revenue base, it also curtailed the fiscal autonomy of states, giving rise to concerns about centralization and the erosion of local control. Over time, federal taxation encroachment expanded, further limiting states' capacity to raise revenue independently and tailor their tax policies to suit local circumstances.

Thesis 80 underscores the importance of reinstating fiscal autonomy to states by granting them exclusive rights to impose permanent income and sales taxes as their respective legislatures see fit. This approach empowers state governments to craft tax policies that resonate with the preferences and priorities of their constituents, fostering innovation, competition, and accountability in governance while ensuring the federal government will not slip into the bad habit of reimposing a permanent income tax. Entrusting the right to a permanent income tax authority to states fosters fiscal responsibility and transparency, as state officials are directly accountable to their constituents for the allocation of tax revenues. By decentralizing tax powers, Thesis 80 seeks to lessen the administrative burden on the federal government and empower states to address their unique fiscal challenges more effectively.

Through the restoration of fiscal autonomy and local governance, this proposal promotes the principles of federalism and enhances accountability and efficiency in government. Granting states and counties exclusive control over permanent income and sales taxes presents a compelling argument. As the United States grapples with complex fiscal issues, a renewed focus on state-level taxation autonomy provides a route to increased flexibility, innovation, and responsiveness in public policy.

THESIS 81

Property taxes should be eradicated in lieu of sales tax on products produced from property and property sales.

Much of this book pertains to how the federal government should be repaired for a more representative republic, but one cannot discuss tax issues without addressing the most pernicious tax that affects the majority of Americans: local property tax. Thesis 81 presents a foundational alteration in taxation policy, proposing that state governments should allow the substitution of property taxes with sales taxes on products originating from property and property sales. This essay analyzes the rationale behind this proposition, leveraging historical context and contemporary economic principles to highlight its significance.

The essence of Thesis 81 lies in recognizing the limitations of traditional property taxes and the potential of sales taxes to stimulate economic growth. By transitioning away from property taxes, governments can create a more conducive environment for investment and promote fairness in taxation.

Across history, property taxes have stood as a principal revenue stream for local governments, tracing their origins back to ancient civilizations. In the United States, property taxes have been instrumental in financing localized public services and the advancement of infrastructure. The original legitimacy for property taxes was rooted in an agricultural society where property meant the means of production; it was akin to a capital tax on potential income. Property ownership was directly tied to one's ability to generate wealth, and taxing it was a logical approach. However, this dependence on property ownership as a taxation foundation has drawn criticism concerning equity and economic efficacy in the modern context.

Thesis 81 advocates for replacing property taxes with sales taxes on property-related transactions, such as property sales and the sale of products derived from property. This shift offers several advantages, including simplification of the tax system, incentivization of investment in real estate, and alignment of taxation with economic activity.

Property tax structures often include mechanisms that assess commercial properties and second homes at higher rates than owner-occupied homes. This differential assessment aims to reflect the presumed higher economic benefit derived from commercial properties and investment-driven residential properties, which are often rented out for income. These properties are typically valued not only on their physical attributes but also on their potential to generate revenue, which can lead to higher assessments compared to primary residences.

This discrepancy in assessment rates means that property investors face significantly higher property taxes. These increased costs are frequently passed down to tenants through raised rents, placing a disproportionate financial burden on low-income renters who may live in these properties. Furthermore, owners of second homes may experience higher tax rates compared to their primary residences, reflecting a policy intent to leverage tax policy for residential stability over investment gains. This system, while designed to target higher income levels and commercial profitability, can inadvertently impact rental affordability, especially in markets where housing supply is limited, and demand is high. Thus, the mechanism of assessing commercial property and second homes at higher rates amplifies the challenges of housing affordability, particularly affecting the most economically vulnerable populations.

By implementing sales taxes on property transactions, local governments can capture revenue from property-related economic activity while maintaining the revenue necessary to fund local services like schools, infrastructure, and first responders.

This reform holds promise for unleashing economic opportunities and encouraging investment. Embracing this transition can enable policymakers to establish the foundation for ongoing economic revitalization and prosperity.

—◆—

Part VII

MY PERSONAL THOUGHTS REGARDING GLOBAL/NATIONAL CORPORATIONS (G/NC)

Concentrated power is not rendered harmless by the good
intentions of those who create it.

—MILTON FRIEDMAN

When plunder becomes a way of life for a group of men in a society,
over the course of time they create for themselves a legal system that authorizes it
and a moral code that glorifies it.

—FRÉDÉRIC BASTIAT

THESIS 82

*The constitution's protection of private property, and ease in establishing
corporations, provide for the unprecedented expansion of individual
entrepreneurialism and a competitive marketplace.*

Understanding the constitutional framework that encourages private property rights and facilitates the formation of businesses is critical to understanding the dynamics of entrepreneurship and economic development. It is obvious to see how these fundamental protections have contributed to the unprecedented rise of the American economy.

The drafting of the United States Constitution in the late 18th century was a watershed milestone in the history of economic governance with the inclusion the Patent and Copyright Clause of the Constitution (found in Article I, Section 8) as well as the 5th Amendment. The Constitution's authors realized that maintaining private property and creative rights was a critical component of individual liberty and economic growth.

The capacity to form corporations allowed entrepreneurs to pool their resources, share risks, and have better access to capital markets. This encouraged the spread of industries like manufacturing, finance, and transportation, resulting in economic growth and wealth creation. The competitive marketplace created as a result of these fundamental principles encouraged entrepreneurship and innovation, resulting in technical improvements and greater productivity. The dynamism of the American economy, typified by creative destruction and market-driven competition, became a signature of the nation's economic success.

THESIS 83

The 18th-century architects of this nation did not anticipate the accumulated power of 21st-century Global/National Corporations, or G/NCs.

Thesis 83 highlights the importance of recognizing that the architects of the 18th century could not have predicted the immense power held by modern corporations. Through an examination of history, we can grasp the development of corporate power dynamics and their impact on governance and society.

During the 18th century, the foundations of modern nation-states were laid, with governance structures primarily focused on regulating commerce and maintaining political stability. However, the framers of these nations could not have predicted the emergence of transnational corporations with unprecedented economic and political influence within a nation that was built on a citizenry primarily made up of farmers and shopkeepers.

Thesis 83 prompts a reflection on the evolution of corporate power from its humble beginnings to its current dominance. Through historical analysis, we can observe the transition from small-scale enterprises to massive conglomerates operating across borders and industries.

The Industrial Revolution marked the beginning of corporate expansion, as advancements in technology and transportation facilitated the growth of large-scale enterprises. Over time, corporations accumulated wealth, resources, and political influence, shaping global economies and challenging the authority of nation-states.

The 21st century witnessed the rise of multinational corporations with unparalleled reach and power. These entities transcend geographical boundaries, operating in multiple jurisdictions while exerting significant influence over governments, economies, and societies worldwide.

As a result of global corporations' unforeseen influence in 21st-century societies, Thesis 83 emphasizes the necessity of dealing with them. Through an examination of historical trends and developments, we gain valuable insights into the origins and consequences of corporate hegemony in the modern era. Looking ahead, it is crucial to critically evaluate the role of corporations in society and ensure that governance mechanisms effectively manage their impact, thereby upholding democratic principles and protecting the welfare of citizens.

THESIS 84

Modern G/NCs have assumed monopolistic power over local populations equal to or surpassing what was traditionally reserved for the government.

Across the annals of history, governments have wielded authority over their populations, overseeing commerce, enforcing laws, and delivering vital services. Yet, the ascent of modern global corporations has disrupted this conventional model, as these entities have amassed considerable economic clout and influence.

Thesis 84 prompts an exploration of the evolution of corporate power and its impact on local populations. Through historical analysis, we can observe parallels between past governmental authority and the monopolistic control exerted by modern G/NCs.

During the Industrial Revolution, governments played a central role in regulating emerging industries and ensuring fair competition. However, as corporations grew in size and scope, they began to wield considerable economic influence, often rivaling or surpassing the power of governments.

In the 20th and 21st centuries, the rise of multinational corporations further eroded government authority, as these entities operated across borders and exerted influence over multiple jurisdictions. Through mergers, acquisitions, and strategic alliances, corporations expanded their reach and consolidated their control over key industries.

Today, modern G/NCs hold unprecedented monopolistic power over local populations, controlling essential goods, services, and resources. This dominance extends to areas such as technology, finance, health care, and agriculture, shaping the daily lives of individuals and communities.

THESIS 85

*Modern monopolistic G/NCs have undermined the economic and
political independence of entrepreneurs to thrive on a local/ state level.*

Throughout the history of our nation, entrepreneurialism has been a driving force behind economic growth and innovation at the local and state levels. Communities relied on local businesses and enterprises to meet their needs, fostering economic diversity and resilience.

Thesis 85 prompts an exploration of how modern G/NCs have disrupted this ecosystem, consolidating economic power and stifling competition from local entrepreneurs. By dominating key industries and markets, these corporations have limited the opportunities for small businesses to thrive and innovate, especially in rural communities.

The political influence wielded by G/NCs has undermined the ability of local governments to enact policies that support entrepreneurship and economic independence. Corporate lobbying and campaign contributions have often resulted in policies that favor the interests of large corporations over those of local businesses and communities.

The concentration of economic power in the hands of a few G/NCs has also limited the ability of local entrepreneurs to compete on a level playing field. These corporations often enjoy preferential treatment in terms of access to resources, markets, and regulatory frameworks, placing smaller businesses at a significant disadvantage.

Several studies have demonstrated that modern monopolistic G/NCs have adverse effects on local entrepreneurialism, economic independence, and political independence. Understanding the challenges communities face when asserting their autonomy in the face of corporate dominance can be gained by studying historical precedents. Moving forward, it is essential to advocate for policies that support local businesses and promote economic diversity and resilience at the grassroots level.

THESIS 86

The centralized monopolistic culture of G/NCs has infiltrated our society, affecting political parties, professional associations, state/federal departments, and regulatory agencies and undermining individualism, free thought, and intellectual competitiveness.

Understanding the impact of centralized monopolistic culture on society is critical to recognizing its consequences for individual autonomy and intellectual diversity. By looking at historical instances, we can learn how monopolistic influences have altered societal norms and institutions throughout time.

Over the course of history, civilizations have struggled with concentrated power and influence in the hands of a few dominant entities. From ancient empires to modern enterprises, centralized control has frequently resulted in the suppression of opposing viewpoints and the stifling of intellectual creativity.

Thesis 86 prompts an exploration of how the monopolistic culture propagated by G/NCs has permeated various sectors of society, including politics, academia, and regulatory bodies. By centralizing power and influence, these corporations have undermined the principles of individualism, free thought, and intellectual competitiveness.

In politics, the influence of corporate lobbying and campaign contributions has led to the prioritization of corporate interests over those of the general public. Political parties often align themselves with corporate agendas, resulting in policies that favor the wealthy and powerful at the expense of ordinary citizens.

Similarly, professional associations and regulatory agencies tasked with upholding standards and promoting innovation have been susceptible to capture by a corporate mindset where adherence to bureaucratic "systems" takes precedence over personal innovation, stifling competition and inhibiting intellectual diversity. The current condition of our public school bureaucracy, the "Uniform Building Code" and how it is promulgated, enacted, and enforced locally and how the government's COVID response minimized alternative viewpoints are the most prominent examples of this debilitating trend.

At the heart of the issue lies a culture that values conformity and compliance over independent thinking and innovation. The monopolistic tendencies of G/NCs have created an environment where dissenting voices are marginalized and alternative viewpoints are suppressed in favor of maintaining the status quo.

Part VIII

WHAT SHOULD WE DO TO LIMIT CORPORATE HEGEMONY?

The greatest way to live with honor in this world is to be what we pretend to be.

—SOCRATES

THESIS 87

Constitutional amendment to distinguish natural persons, or individual citizens, from artificial personas, or corporations.

THESIS 88

Ensure the 14th Amendment refers to "natural persons."

As a result of the U.S. Supreme Court decision in the *Citizens United* case, we need to examine the historical evolution of legal personality as well as the critical need for a clear line of distinction between different types of entities.

A clear distinction between natural persons and artificial personas is critical to ensuring legal systems' transparency, accountability, and fairness. Through a study of historical precedents and contemporary issues, it is imperative we justify the urgency of a constitutional change to set clear boundaries between these legal concepts.

Legal personhood has evolved over millennia, with older legal systems acknowledging individuals as the principal recipients of rights and obligations. However, the rise of corporations in the contemporary age complicated this paradigm, blurring the distinction between natural and artificial entities.

During the Industrial Revolution, corporations gained prominence, leading to debates over their legal status and rights. In landmark cases such as *Dartmouth College v. Woodward* (1819), the Supreme Court of the United States affirmed corporations' rights as artificial persons, capable of entering contracts and holding property.

As corporations expanded in influence and scope, concerns arose regarding their accountability and responsibility. The lack of a clear demarcation between natural persons and artificial personas muddied legal proceedings, making it difficult to hold companies accountable for their conduct. The Gilded Age monopolies and the Great Depression demonstrate the dangers of unfettered corporate dominance. In response, regulatory measures such as the Sherman Antitrust Act (1890) and the Securities Act of 1933 were enacted to limit monopolistic activities and safeguard customers.

However, as corporate law evolved and international firms proliferated in the twentieth and twenty-first centuries, the legal landscape became even more difficult. The 2010 decision in *Citizens United*, which allowed corporations to spend limitless amounts on political elections, highlighted the need for clarity in defining legal personhood.

A constitutional amendment to distinguish natural persons from artificial personas is imperative for safeguarding democratic principles and ensuring equitable governance. By establishing clear boundaries between individual citizens and corporate entities, the legal system can uphold accountability, transparency, and the rights of all and return our nation to one for "we the people" as originally intended and not "we the corporations."

The 14th Amendment, ratified in 1868, was a pivotal moment in American history, designed to protect the rights of newly freed slaves by ensuring equal protection under the law. Its primary clauses include the Citizenship Clause, the Due Process Clause, and the Equal Protection Clause.

The initial objective was to ensure that no state could violate fundamental rights of citizens, particularly the most recently freed slaves, in the aftermath of the Civil War. Initially, the 14th Amendment was lauded for its role in furthering civil rights and creating a legal foundation for mitigating racial discrimination. However, its meaning has evolved in unexpected ways over time. One notable transition happened in the late 19th and early 20th centuries, when the Supreme Court began to apply the amendment's protections to businesses.

The landmark case of *Santa Clara County v. Southern Pacific Railroad* (1886) is often cited as the origin of corporate personhood. Although the decision did not explicitly grant corporations 14th Amendment rights, a headnote by the court reporter indicated that the Court recognized corporations as "persons" under the amendment. This interpretation set a precedent for subsequent rulings, leading to an era where corporations could claim the same rights as individual citizens.

The extension of 14th Amendment rights to corporations has had profound implications for American society. Corporations, driven by profit motives, have leveraged these rights to influence politics, evade regulations, and prioritize their interests over those of the general public. The *Citizens United* ruling, which allowed unlimited corporate spending in political campaigns, exemplifies the problematic nature of corporate personhood.

This decision has led to a significant influx of corporate money in politics, undermining the democratic process and diluting the voices of individual citizens. The influence of corporations on politics and society has been significant. During the Gilded Age, powerful industrialists and their corporations wielded immense power, often at the expense of workers' rights and environmental sustainability. The monopolistic practices of corporations like Standard Oil and U.S. Steel stifled competition and exploited labor, prompting government intervention through antitrust laws.

More recently, the 2008 financial crisis highlighted the dangers of unchecked corporate power. Financial institutions, operating with minimal oversight, engaged in risky behaviors that ultimately led to a global economic meltdown. The subsequent government bailouts underscored the influence of corporations on public policy, as taxpayer money was used to rescue entities deemed "too big to fail" with the implied notion that the individual citizens and families who lost their homes were "too small to succeed."

By restoring the original intent of the 14th Amendment, we can safeguard the rights of individual citizens and promote democratic values. This would mark a significant milestone in the ongoing effort to balance the interests of individuals and corporations within the framework of American democracy.

THESIS 89

Establishment of, and rigid enforcement of, antitrust laws in both the state and national marketplace with a prioritized focus on media and medical conglomerates.

The establishment and rigid enforcement of antitrust laws are critical to maintaining a fair and competitive marketplace, especially in smaller communities. Antitrust laws, designed to prevent monopolies and promote competition, have been a cornerstone of American economic policy since the late 19th century. These laws are intended to prohibit practices that restrain trade, prevent price-fixing, and ensure that markets remain competitive. The ultimate goal is to protect consumers, foster innovation, encourage community-based entrepreneurs and local investment, and prevent the concentration of economic power in the hands of a few entities.

The origins of antitrust legislation in the United States can be traced back to the Sherman Antitrust Act of 1890. This landmark law was enacted in response to the monopolistic practices of large corporations, such as Standard Oil and the railroads, which stifled competition, exploited low wage workers, and manipulated consumers. The Act aimed to prohibit anti-competitive agreements and unilateral conduct that monopolized or attempted to monopolize trade or commerce.

Subsequent legislation, including the Clayton Antitrust Act of 1914 and the Federal Trade Commission Act of 1914, further strengthened antitrust enforcement by addressing specific practices and establishing regulatory bodies to oversee and enforce these laws. Together, these acts provided a framework for promoting competition and curbing monopolistic behavior.

In recent decades, the media and health care industries have undergone significant consolidation, leading to the rise of powerful conglomerates with substantial market influence. This consolidation poses unique challenges and underscores the need for vigilant antitrust enforcement.

The media landscape has seen the emergence of a few dominant players controlling vast networks of television stations, newspapers, and digital platforms. Companies like Comcast, Disney, and News Corp have acquired numerous smaller entities, creating conglomerates with significant control over information dissemination and advertising revenue.

In the 1950s and 60s, the "trusted" media landscape of Walter Cronkite and David Brinkley and Mike Wallace has been referred to as the golden age when America trusted what our favorite news anchors were telling us every night. During this period, a handful of major national networks, such as CBS, NBC, and ABC, dominated the broadcast industry, creating a relatively uniform source of news for the American public. The Federal Communications Commission played a crucial role in regulating these monopolistic networks, emphasizing the need for broadcasters to serve the public interest, which included providing objective and reliable news coverage. This regulatory environment, coupled with the counterbalance of the numerous privately owned distributors and affiliates across the nation who created local market content independently, contributed to a sense of trust and credibility in the news being delivered.

However, the landscape began to shift as profit motives increasingly influenced the content and presentation of news. With the advent of television, news programs became more entertainment-oriented to attract larger audiences and higher advertising revenues. The introduction of the Fairness Doctrine in 1949, which required broadcasters to present contrasting viewpoints on controversial issues, initially helped maintain a level of balance and objectivity. Nevertheless, as competition for viewers intensified, networks started prioritizing sensational stories and dramatic presentation styles to boost ratings, often at the expense of nuanced and thorough reporting. This shift toward profit-driven news marked the beginning of the erosion of purely objective journalism.

The demise of objective news can be traced to several key factors and legislative changes. The repeal of the Fairness Doctrine in 1987 removed the obligation for broadcasters to present balanced viewpoints, allowing for more partisan and biased reporting. Additionally, the Telecommunications Act of 1996 further deregulated the media industry, leading to greater consolidation of localized media ownership. This consolidation resulted in fewer, larger corporations controlling a vast majority of the media landscape, often prioritizing their corporate interests over localized journalistic integrity. The rise of 24-hour news channels and the internet also fragmented the audience, driving outlets to cater to specific demographics and political leanings, further polarizing news coverage and undermining the trust in media that had been established in previous decades.

Though there has been a proliferation of national news companies beyond the old "Big Three," the concentration of localized media ownership has reduced diversity of viewpoints, the potential for biased reporting, and the erosion of local journalism. Instead of a well-regulated big three national broadcast companies mitigated by hundreds of local media outlets, there are now only six media outlets that own 90% of media outlets, including print media. The power wielded by these conglomerates can shape public opinion, influence political processes, and destroy the ability for local communities to access good quality unbiased news delivery.

The health care sector has experienced substantial consolidation, with large hospital chains, pharmaceutical companies, and insurance providers dominating the market. This consolidation has led to higher health care costs, diminished incentives for innovation, and reduced access to services, especially in our rural communities.

The merger of large pharmaceutical companies has limited competition, resulting in fewer choices for consumers and higher prices for medications. Additionally, the integration of health care providers and insurance companies can create conflicts of interest and reduce the quality of patient care. Robust antitrust enforcement is essential to prevent these conglomerates from exploiting their market power and to ensure that health care remains affordable, innovative, and accessible.

Parallel with the trend for centralization of health care services, we have seen an alarming drop in citizens choosing to become primary care physicians.

According to American Medical Association President Jesse M. Ehrenfeld, M.D., MPH, in an address to the National Press Club in 2023, this issue needs urgent attention.

Below is a partial list of his reasons why:

- An increasingly impersonal and bureaucratic health care system that places enormous administrative hassles and burdens in our lap each day and leaves us feeling powerless to make any meaningful change.

- Physicians today, on average, spend about two hours on paperwork for every one hour we spend with patients.

- An attack on science that undermines trust in our medical institutions, and too often leads to threats and hostility directed at us and other health care workers.

- Government intrusion into health care decisions and aggressive efforts in many states to criminalize care supported by science and evidence.

- Increasing consolidation across health care that is giving more power to our nation's largest hospitals, health systems, and insurers, and less autonomy and fewer choices to patients and doctors.
- Widening health disparities for historically marginalized communities, by race and by gender, between wealthy and low-income, and people living in urban and rural settings.
- And for the last 20 years, a shrinking Medicare reimbursement rate for physicians that has pushed many small, independent practices to the brink of financial collapse and jeopardized care for millions of America's seniors.

Of all the issues facing our rural communities, this one is going to lead us to catastrophic results.

To address the challenges posed by modern media and medical conglomerates, it is imperative to prioritize the enforcement of antitrust laws. This requires a multifaceted approach, including:

Updating Legislation: Modernizing antitrust laws to address the complexities of the digital age and the unique challenges posed by technological advancements, like artificial intelligence, and globalization.

Collaboration with States: Encouraging state governments to enact and enforce their own antitrust laws, complementing federal efforts and addressing local market dynamics.

The establishment and rigid enforcement of antitrust laws are essential to maintaining a fair and competitive marketplace, particularly in the media and health care sectors. By prioritizing these efforts, we can ensure that media and medical conglomerates do not undermine competition, exploit consumers, or stifle innovation.

THESIS 90

The federal government should be prohibited to intervene in an individual's right to self-medicate.

This thesis is a contentious yet crucial aspect of personal liberty and autonomy. The right to self-medicate encompasses the freedom for individuals to make decisions about their own health and treatment options without undue interference from the government. This principle is rooted in the broader concept of personal autonomy and the belief that individuals have the inherent right to control their own bodies and health choices.

The struggle for medical autonomy has been a recurring theme in many societies. From the early days of patent medicines in the 19th century to the more recent debates over medical marijuana and alternative therapies, the right to self-medicate has often clashed with government regulations and pharmaceutical interests.

In the 19th and early 20th centuries, patent medicines were widely available and often marketed with little to no regulation. These remedies, while sometimes effective, could also be dangerous or fraudulent. The rise of patent medicines eventually led to the establishment of regulatory bodies like the Food and Drug Administration to ensure the safety and efficacy of pharmaceuticals. While these regulations were necessary to protect public health, they also marked the beginning of increased government intervention in individual health choices.

The legalization of medical marijuana in various states serves as a modern example of the tension between federal authority and individual rights to self-medicate. Despite substantial evidence supporting the medical benefits of cannabis for conditions like chronic pain and epilepsy, federal law continues to classify marijuana as a Schedule I controlled substance, making it illegal at the federal level. This conflict has led to significant legal and political battles, highlighting the complex dynamics between state autonomy, federal regulation, and individual rights.

Personal Autonomy: At the core of this principle is the belief that individuals should have the ultimate authority over their own bodies and health decisions. This includes the right to choose their own treatments, whether conventional or alternative.

Innovation and Access: Allowing individuals the freedom to self-medicate can spur innovation in health care by encouraging the exploration of alternative therapies and treatments. It can also increase access to treatments that may not be readily available through conventional medical channels.

Historical Precedents: Historical examples demonstrate that excessive regulation can stifle individual freedom and limit access to potentially beneficial treatments. The evolution of drug regulation shows a pattern where individual autonomy is often sacrificed in the name of public safety, sometimes to the detriment of personal liberty.

While the prohibition of federal intervention in self-medication rights is compelling, it is not without challenges:

Public Safety: One of the primary roles of government regulation is to protect public health. Unregulated self-medication can lead to the misuse of substances, potentially causing harm to individuals and society.

Quality and Efficacy: Ensuring that medications are safe and effective is a legitimate concern. Without regulation, there is a risk of widespread use of ineffective or dangerous treatments.

Legal and Ethical Issues: The legal framework surrounding drug use and distribution is complex. Balancing individual rights with the need to prevent abuse and ensure public safety requires careful consideration.

For these reasons the government best suited to deal with this problem is the government closest to the people: the states.

The ongoing opioid crisis in the United States serves as a cautionary tale about the dangers of unregulated access to powerful medications. The overprescription and misuse of opioids have led to widespread addiction and overdose deaths, illustrating the potential risks of self-medication without appropriate oversight.

Conversely, the successful push for the legalization of medical marijuana in many states demonstrates the positive outcomes of allowing individuals more control over their treatment options. Patients with conditions like cancer, HIV/AIDS, and chronic pain have benefitted significantly from access to cannabis, highlighting the potential benefits of reduced federal intervention.

The prohibition of federal law intervening in individuals' right to self-medicate is a principle that underscores the importance of personal autonomy and the right to control one's own health decisions. While there are significant challenges and risks associated with unregulated self-medication, historical examples show that excessive regulation can also impede access to beneficial treatments, stifle innovation, and erode personal liberty. Balancing these concerns requires a nuanced approach that respects individual rights while ensuring public safety.

THESIS 91

Institute rank choice or approval voting for federal office

The principle of instituting rank choice or approval voting for federal office is a significant reform with profound implications for the democratic process.

Voting reform is crucial for ensuring that electoral outcomes accurately reflect the will of the people. Traditional plurality voting systems often result in winners who lack majority support and can discourage voter participation and perpetuate a polarized political environment. Rank choice and approval voting systems offer alternative methods designed to enhance democratic fairness and representation.

The plurality voting system, also known as "first-past-the-post," has long been the standard in U.S. federal elections. This system awards victory to the candidate with the most votes, regardless of whether they achieve a majority. Historical examples highlight the limitations and unintended consequences of this approach.

The 1912 Presidential Election: This election featured incumbent President William Howard Taft, former President Theodore Roosevelt, and Democrat Woodrow Wilson. Roosevelt's entry as a Progressive Party candidate split the Republican vote, enabling Wilson to win with only 42% of the popular vote. This outcome illustrated how plurality voting can result in a leader who lacks broad support, as the combined votes for Taft and Roosevelt far exceeded those for Wilson.

The 2000 Presidential Election: The contentious election between George W. Bush and Al Gore was notably influenced by third-party candidate Ralph Nader. Nader's candidacy drew votes away from Gore, particularly in key states like Florida, where the margin of victory was razor-thin. The plurality system did not account for voters' preferences beyond their first choice, contributing to a highly divisive and disputed outcome.

Rank choice voting (RCV), also known as instant-runoff voting, allows voters to rank candidates in order of preference. If no candidate secures a majority in the initial count, the candidate with the fewest votes is eliminated, and their votes are redistributed based on second preferences. This process continues until a candidate achieves a majority.

This system has promoted a more nuanced and representative electoral outcome, reducing the likelihood of extreme partisanship and encouraging more candidates to participate.

San Francisco and Maine: In the United States, several cities and the state of Maine have adopted RCV for various elections. In San Francisco, RCV has led to more diverse representation and less negative campaigning, as candidates seek to gain second- and third-choice votes. Maine's use of RCV in federal elections has similarly promoted greater voter engagement and satisfaction with the electoral process.

Approval voting allows voters to select (approve) any number of candidates they find acceptable. The candidate with the highest number of approvals wins. This system can diminish the "spoiler effect" of third-party candidates and encourages a broader spectrum of candidates to run.

Dartmouth College: Dartmouth College has used approval voting for alumni trustee elections since 1990. The system has led to more inclusive and representative outcomes, as voters are not forced to choose a single candidate but can express support for all acceptable options.

Fargo, North Dakota: In 2018, Fargo became the first U.S. city to implement approval voting for local elections. The initial elections under this system have shown increased voter satisfaction and a more accurate reflection of voter preferences.

ENHANCING DEMOCRATIC LEGITIMACY

Both RCV and approval voting ensure that elected officials have broader support from their constituents. By requiring a majority (in the case of RCV) or allowing multiple approvals, these systems better reflect the electorate's will. This leads to greater legitimacy for elected officials and can reduce political polarization.

ENCOURAGING POSITIVE CAMPAIGNING

With RCV, candidates are incentivized to seek broader appeal to gain second- and third-choice votes, often leading to more positive and issue-focused campaigns. Similarly, approval voting encourages candidates to seek approval from a wider audience, reducing negative campaigning and promoting coalition-building.

REDUCING THE SPOILER EFFECT

Both systems address the spoiler effect, where third-party or independent candidates split the vote, potentially leading to an outcome not reflective of the majority's preference. By accommodating multiple preferences (RCV) or approvals, these systems mitigate the impact of vote splitting and encourage more diverse candidacies.

The implementation of rank choice or approval voting for federal office represents a crucial step toward a more representative and functional democracy. Elections around the world and within the United States demonstrate the effectiveness of these systems in producing fairer electoral outcomes, enhancing democratic legitimacy, and encouraging positive political engagement. By reforming the way we vote, we can ensure that our elected officials truly represent the will of the people, fostering a healthier and more inclusive political landscape.

THESIS 92

Prohibit straight ticket voting along party lines.

The principle of prohibiting straight ticket voting along party lines is a crucial reform with significant implications for the democratic process. Straight ticket voting, where a voter selects all candidates from a single party with one mark on the ballot, simplifies the voting process but can lead to a range of issues. It can perpetuate party loyalty over individual candidate merit, reduce voter engagement with specific issues, and contribute to political polarization. Prohibiting this practice encourages voters to make more informed decisions, potentially leading to a more accountable and representative government.

Straight ticket voting has a long history in the United States, dating back to the 19th century. Originally, it was a product of party dominance and the influence of political machines. Over time, it became a tool for maintaining party control and simplifying the voting process for the electorate. However, the drawbacks of this system have become increasingly apparent.

Political Machines and Party Dominance: In the late 19th and early 20th centuries, political machines, such as Tammany Hall in New York

City, wielded significant power. These organizations encouraged straight ticket voting to ensure their preferred candidates were elected at all levels of government. While this practice streamlined voting, it also entrenched corruption and reduced accountability.

Mid-20th-Century Reform Movements: During the mid-20th century, reform movements aimed at reducing the power of political machines and increasing voter engagement began to take hold. These movements recognized that straight ticket voting contributed to a lack of individual candidate scrutiny and promoted the continuation of party-controlled politics.

Texas 2018 Midterm Elections: In the 2018 midterm elections, Texas saw a high level of straight ticket voting, with nearly two-thirds of voters using this option. This trend demonstrated the strong party loyalty among voters but also highlighted the risk of voters not fully considering individual candidates' qualifications and positions.

Michigan's Shift in 2016: Michigan eliminated straight ticket voting for the 2016 elections. This change was intended to encourage voters to consider each candidate on the ballot. However, it also led to longer wait times at polling places, indicating the need for additional voter education and resources to support this transition.

ENCOURAGING INFORMED VOTING

By prohibiting straight ticket voting, voters are encouraged to evaluate each candidate on their own merits. This shift promotes a more informed electorate that is more likely to consider the specific qualifications, policies, and track records of individual candidates. It helps to reduce blind party loyalty and increase accountability.

REDUCING POLITICAL POLARIZATION

Straight ticket voting can exacerbate political polarization by reinforcing party divisions. When voters are required to make individual selections for each office, they may be more likely to support candidates from different parties based on their positions on various issues. This practice can lead to a more nuanced and less polarized political landscape.

INCREASING ACCOUNTABILITY

Candidates who are elected through a system that prohibits straight ticket voting are more likely to be held accountable for their actions and policies. Without the safety net of party loyalty, these candidates must appeal directly to voters based on their performance and positions. This accountability can lead to better governance and more responsive representatives.

North Carolina's 2013 Reform: North Carolina eliminated straight ticket voting in 2013. The change was part of a broader effort to modernize the state's voting system and encourage greater voter engagement with individual races. The reform faced criticism for potentially increasing voter confusion, but it also aimed to promote more thoughtful voting.

Wisconsin's Voter Education Efforts: When Wisconsin eliminated straight ticket voting, the state invested in voter education campaigns to help citizens understand the new system. These efforts included informational materials and public service announcements, demonstrating the importance of supporting voters through such transitions.

The prohibition of straight ticket voting along party lines is a crucial reform for enhancing the democratic process. By examining historical examples, it is evident that this practice can contribute to party dominance, reduce voter engagement, and exacerbate political polarization. Prohibiting straight ticket voting encourages voters to make more informed decisions, increases accountability for elected officials, and promotes a more nuanced and less polarized political landscape. As we move forward, implementing this reform can help create a more representative and responsive government, ultimately strengthening the democratic foundation of our society.

THESIS 93

Prohibit local/state/federal administrative support
for political party primaries.

In a democratic society, the integrity and fairness of the electoral process are paramount. One significant aspect of maintaining this integrity is ensuring that government resources are not disproportionately used to favor any political party. Political party primaries are the processes by which parties select their candidates for various public offices. While these primaries are essential for party organization and candidate selection, the involvement of government resources in supporting them can lead to unfair advantages, misuse of public funds, and erosion of public trust in the electoral system. By prohibiting administrative support for these primaries, we can promote a more equitable and transparent political process.

In the early years of the United States, political parties were not as entrenched as they are today. The Founding Fathers, including George Washington, expressed concerns about the divisive nature of political parties. Over time, however, parties became a central feature of American politics. Primaries emerged as a means for parties to democratize their candidate selection processes, moving away from the earlier caucus systems that were often controlled by a few influential individuals.

By the early 20th century, primary elections had become widespread in the United States. These primaries were initially seen as a way to give more power to party members and reduce corruption. However, the administration and funding of these primaries often fell to local, state, and federal governments, raising concerns about the appropriate use of public resources.

Chicago's 1968 Democratic National Convention: The 1968 Democratic National Convention in Chicago highlighted the issues that can arise when government resources are used to support party activities. The heavy police presence and use of city resources during the convention led to widespread criticism and highlighted the potential for misuse of public funds in partisan activities.

Florida's 2000 Presidential Primary: The Florida primary in 2000 was marked by significant controversy, including issues with ballot design and counting. The involvement of state resources in administering the primary led to questions about the fairness and impartiality of the process, underscoring the need for clear boundaries between government functions and party activities.

PROMOTING FAIRNESS AND EQUITY

By prohibiting government support for political party primaries, we ensure that no party receives an unfair advantage using public resources. This promotes a level playing field where parties must rely on their own resources and organizational capabilities, rather than taxpayer-funded support.

PRESERVING PUBLIC TRUST

Public trust in the electoral system is crucial for the functioning of a healthy democracy. When government resources are used to support party primaries, it can lead to perceptions of bias and favoritism. Prohibiting this practice helps to maintain the integrity of the electoral process and ensures that public funds are used appropriately.

ENCOURAGING PARTY RESPONSIBILITY

Political parties should be responsible for organizing and funding their own candidate selection processes. This responsibility encourages parties to develop robust organizational structures and engage more actively with their members. It also reduces the burden on government agencies and allows them to focus on administering general elections impartially.

California's Proposition 14 (2010): In 2010, California voters approved

Proposition 14, which established a "top-two" primary system. This reform aimed to reduce party influence and increase voter choice. While not a direct prohibition of government support for party primaries, it represented a significant shift toward reducing the role of parties in the primary process.

Nebraska's Nonpartisan Legislature: Nebraska's unique unicameral legislature is officially nonpartisan. Primary elections for state legislative seats do not involve party affiliation, demonstrating a successful model of reducing party influence in the electoral process. This system underscores the potential benefits of separating party activities from government functions.

Prohibiting local, state, and federal administrative support for political party primaries is a crucial reform for ensuring the fairness and integrity of the electoral process. Historical examples illustrate the potential for misuse of public resources and the importance of maintaining a clear separation between government functions and party activities. By implementing this reform, we can promote a more equitable political landscape, preserve public trust in the electoral system, and encourage political parties to take greater responsibility for their own candidate selection processes.

THESIS 94

Prohibit any person holding federal position (elected or employee) from joining the board of a corporation or being hired as executive leadership in a corporation for a time period equal to their most recent time in office/employment.

The relationship between government officials and the private sector has long been a subject of intense scrutiny and debate. The proposal to prohibit any natural person holding a federal position—whether elected or employed— from joining the board of a corporation or being hired as executive leadership in a corporation for a period equal to their most recent time in office or employment is a measure designed to address potential conflicts of interest and the influence of corporate power on public policy.

The essence of this proposal lies in ensuring that government officials remain impartial and dedicated to public service without the undue influence of private sector interests. By preventing federal officials from immediately transitioning into high-ranking corporate roles, this measure aims to mitigate the risk of conflicts of interest, enhance public trust in government, and ensure that policy decisions are made in the public interest rather than for private gain.

The "revolving door" between government service and the private sector is a well-documented phenomenon. Historically, many officials have leveraged their public service experience and connections to secure lucrative positions in the corporate world. This practice has raised concerns about the integrity of government decisions and the potential for regulatory capture, where industries exert undue influence over the agencies meant to regulate them.

One of the earliest examples of concern over the revolving door can be traced back to the post-Civil War era, when former government officials, particularly those involved in railroad regulation, transitioned into positions within the very companies they once oversaw. This led to widespread public suspicion and calls for greater oversight and transparency.

During the Gilded Age and Progressive Era (late 19th and early 20th centuries), the intertwining of corporate interests and government was particularly pronounced. Powerful industrialists, known as "robber barons," had significant influence over government policies. The close ties between business and government officials led to a series of reforms aimed at curbing corporate power and ensuring government accountability, such as the Sherman Antitrust Act of 1890 and the creation of regulatory bodies like the Interstate Commerce Commission.

In the modern era, the influence of corporate interests on government has continued to be a concern. High-profile cases, such as that of former Secretary of Defense and then Vice President Dick Cheney, who served as CEO of

Halliburton before his tenure as vice president, have been appropriately criticized for the company's significant contracts during the Iraq War, which some argued benefited from Cheney's former connections. Support work for U.S. military operations and U.S.-funded reconstruction projects made up $2.1 billion of the company's $5.5 billion of revenue in the first quarter of 2004, and also contributed $32 million of operating profit to Halliburton.

Lloyd Austin became the first Black secretary of defense after the Senate confirmed him to the post on January 22, 2022. Austin served in the U.S. Army from 1975 to 2012. During his stint as head of U.S. forces in Iraq, Austin befriended President Joe Biden's son, Beau. Austin was then nominated to become the Army's vice chief of staff. Just a year later, then-President Barack Obama tapped Austin to head up U.S. Central Command.

After the election of former President Donald Trump in 2016, Austin left the public sector and assumed positions on the corporate boards of steel manufacturing giant Nucor Corporation, Tenet Healthcare, and United Technologies, which merged with defense contractor Raytheon Company in 2020. The merged corporation, Raytheon Technologies, is among the top five lobbying spenders in the defense sector and spent almost $11 million on lobbying in 2020. According to *Foreign Policy* magazine, Austin earned seven figures from the defense companies. He stepped down from all three board positions following his nomination in 2020. Prior to joining the Biden administration, Austin worked alongside fellow cabinet member and Secretary of State to President Biden, Antony Blinken, at Pine Island Capital Partners, a private equity firm investing in defense companies that touted its access to Washington.

ENHANCING PUBLIC TRUST

Public trust in government is crucial for the effective functioning of a democracy. By implementing a mandatory cooling-off period before federal officials can transition into corporate roles, this proposal seeks to reassure the public that government decisions are made without the prospect of personal financial gain. This can help to rebuild confidence in the integrity and impartiality of public servants.

MITIGATING CONFLICTS OF INTEREST

Conflicts of interest can arise when officials are influenced by the prospect of future employment in the private sector. By prohibiting immediate transitions into corporate leadership roles, this measure reduces the likelihood that officials will make decisions while in office with an eye toward their future career prospects, ensuring that their actions remain focused on serving the public good.

ENCOURAGING DEDICATION TO PUBLIC SERVICE

This proposal also reinforces the principle that public service should be motivated by a commitment to the common good rather than by potential personal gain. It emphasizes that serving in government is a unique responsibility that should not be immediately leveraged for private sector advantage.

THE ETHICS IN GOVERNMENT ACT OF 1978

In response to the Watergate scandal and subsequent concerns about government ethics, the Ethics in Government Act of 1978 introduced various measures to increase transparency and accountability in government. This included post-employment restrictions for federal employees to prevent conflicts of interest. While these measures were a step in the right direction, the proposed prohibition on immediate corporate roles would go further in addressing the revolving door issue.

THESIS 95

Prohibit any candidate or holder of federal or state elected office, or, any person who holds a regulatory position with state or federal government, from investing in publicly held corporations.

This proposal aims to prevent conflicts of interest and ensure that public officials act in the best interest of the citizens they serve rather than being influenced by their personal financial interests. By restricting public officials from investing in publicly held corporations, the proposal seeks to eliminate any potential for corruption, promote transparency, and bolster public trust in government institutions.

EARLY EFFORTS TO ADDRESS CONFLICTS OF INTEREST

The concern over conflicts of interest is not new. Historically, efforts to address such issues have been part of broader attempts to ensure ethical governance. One of the earliest examples in American history can be traced back to the late 18th and early 19th centuries when the fledgling U.S. government sought to establish norms and practices that would prevent the undue influence of private interests on public policy.

During the Progressive Era in the late 19th and early 20th centuries, there was a significant push to curb the influence of big business on government. Reformers sought to address the rampant corruption and conflicts of interest that had become endemic during the Gilded Age. Measures such as the Sherman Antitrust Act of 1890 and the establishment of regulatory bodies like the Federal Trade Commission were steps toward reducing corporate influence on politics and ensuring fair competition.

CASE STUDIES AND EXAMPLES

Several high-profile cases highlight the potential dangers of allowing public officials to hold investments in publicly held corporations. For example, during the 2008 financial crisis, there were numerous instances where lawmakers' financial interests in certain industries appeared to influence their policy decisions. These conflicts of interest undermined public confidence in the government's ability to act impartially.

The Watergate scandal of the 1970s underscored the need for comprehensive ethics reforms. In the aftermath of the scandal, the Ethics in Government Act of 1978 was enacted, introducing significant changes aimed at increasing transparency and accountability among public officials. While the act did not specifically prohibit investments in publicly held corporations, it laid the groundwork for stricter regulations and oversight.

THE INFLUENCE OF CORPORATE LOBBYING

In contemporary politics, corporate lobbying remains a powerful force. Public officials who have financial stakes in publicly held corporations may face pressure to enact policies favorable to those companies, leading to potential conflicts of interest. This influence can skew policy decisions away from the public good and toward the interests of a few powerful entities.

THE NEED FOR STRICTER REGULATIONS

Despite existing regulations, the potential for conflicts of interest persists. The proposal to prohibit public officials from investing in publicly held corporations represents a necessary step toward addressing these ongoing challenges. By eliminating the possibility of personal financial gain from corporate investments, this measure seeks to ensure that public officials remain focused on serving the public interest.

ENHANCING PUBLIC TRUST

Public trust in government is essential for the effective functioning of democracy. By prohibiting investments in publicly held corporations, this proposal aims to reassure the public that their elected officials and regulators are making decisions based solely on the public good, free from personal financial motives.

PROMOTING ETHICAL GOVERNANCE

This proposal supports the principle of ethical governance by ensuring that public officials do not have divided loyalties. When officials are barred from investing in publicly held corporations, they are less likely to face situations where their financial interests conflict with their duty to serve the public.

REDUCING CORRUPTION

The prohibition on investments in publicly held corporations helps to reduce the risk of corruption. Without the opportunity for personal financial gain through corporate investments, public officials are less likely to be influenced by corporate interests, thereby fostering a more honest and transparent government.

LESSONS FROM OTHER COUNTRIES

Several countries have implemented strict regulations to prevent conflicts of interest among public officials. For example, in some European nations, elected officials and high-ranking civil servants are required to divest themselves of any investments that could pose a conflict of interest. These measures have been effective in promoting transparency and maintaining public trust in government institutions.

The United States has seen various efforts to address conflicts of interest through legislation and ethical guidelines. The proposal to prohibit public officials from investing in publicly held corporations builds on this tradition, seeking to further strengthen the integrity of public service and prevent the undue influence of private interests. The proposal to prohibit any candidate for or holder of federal or state elected office, or any individual in a regulatory position with state or federal government, from investing in publicly held corporations is a crucial step toward ensuring ethical governance and maintaining public trust.

CONCLUSION

AS WE REACH THE CONCLUSION of *95 Theses for a Free Republic*, it is clear that the path forward is neither simple nor swift. These theses are not just statements but a call to action, demanding a collective effort to address the multifaceted challenges facing our nation. They are designed to spark dialogue, inspire reflection, and guide our steps toward meaningful reform.

In drafting these theses, my goal has been to initiate a national conversation about the principles and values that should guide us as a republic. Just as Martin Luther's 95 Theses ignited a movement that reshaped the course of history, I hope that this work will serve as a catalyst for a new era of civic engagement and purposeful citizenship.

Implementing these ideas will require patience, persistence, and a commitment to building consensus across our diverse society. Some changes may come quickly, providing immediate benefits and demonstrating progress. However, the most profound and lasting reforms will take time, requiring us to work together, learn from each other, and remain steadfast in our dedication to the common good.

The essence of our republic lies in its people and their shared commitment to liberty, justice, and democracy. By reconnecting with the foundational principles that have sustained us since our founding, we can ensure that future generations inherit a nation that remains true to its ideals. This is not just about preserving our past but about building a future where freedom and opportunity are available to all.

The call to action is not just to implement these theses but to vigorously debate them. An intentional conversation is the whole purpose of this book. Such dialogue must happen in an open society like ours before any new laws are implemented. This process of debate and discussion is essential to ensuring that any actions taken are well-considered, widely supported, and truly beneficial for our nation.

As we move forward, let us remember that the strength of our republic depends on the active participation and vigilance of its citizens. Each of us has a role to play in shaping the direction of our country. Together, we can revive the spirit of intentional citizenship and work toward a brighter future.

Thank you for joining me on this journey. Let us now take these theses and turn them into action, ensuring that our republic remains free, vibrant, and resilient for generations to come.

We do have a republic worth keeping.

Michael Sedenbayl

June 1, 2024
Prosperity, South Carolina

WASHINGTONS FAREWELL ADDRESS

GEORGE WASHINGTON'S FAREWELL ADDRESS IS a historic document that was penned as Washington prepared to leave the presidency after serving two terms. By 1796, George Washington was concluding his second term as the first President of the United States. He had initially wanted to retire after his first term but was persuaded to serve a second term to help stabilize the young nation. Washington was eager to return to private life and his estate at Mount Vernon, as he had served in public life for many years and felt the weight of his age and health.

Washington sought advice from close confidants in drafting his Farewell Address. Alexander Hamilton, his former Secretary of the Treasury, played a significant role in the writing process. James Madison, who had helped with Washington's earlier drafts, also contributed ideas, particularly for a draft prepared in 1792 when Washington first considered retiring. The Address reflected Washington's thoughts on the emerging political landscape, his concerns about factionalism, and his vision for the nation's future. Key themes included the dangers of political parties, the importance of national unity, and the value of neutrality in foreign affairs.

The Farewell Address was not delivered as a speech but published as an open letter to the American people. It appeared in the American Daily

Advertiser, a Philadelphia newspaper, on September 19, 1796. The Address was widely circulated and read across the country, becoming an influential and enduring document in American political thought. Washington warned against the divisive effects of political parties, believing they would lead to factions and weaken the government. He advised against forming permanent alliances with foreign nations, advocating for a policy of neutrality to avoid entanglements in European conflicts. Emphasizing the importance of unity among the states, Washington called for Americans to prioritize their common national identity over regional interests. He also stressed the significance of religion and morality as foundational principles for the country's political prosperity and civic virtue.

Washington's Farewell Address has been cited throughout American history by various leaders and remains a foundational document reflecting the principles and concerns of the early Republic. The Address is still studied and referenced for its insights into the nature of American democracy, the role of government, and the challenges of maintaining unity and liberty.

Its time we return this important founding document to the forefront of our collective conscience for its absence over the past century has compromised our civic engagement.

Below is the address in its original form as printed in The American Daily Advertiser on September 19, 1796. I have highlighted the portions that were utilized as inspiration for 37 of my 95 Theses.

FRIENDS AND CITIZENS:

The period for a new election of a citizen to administer the executive government of the United States being not far distant, and the time actually arrived when your thoughts must be employed in designating the person who is to be clothed with that important trust, it appears to me proper, especially as it may conduce to a more distinct expression of the public voice, that I should now apprise you of the resolution I have formed, to decline being considered among the number of those out of whom a choice is to be made.

I beg you, at the same time, to do me the justice to be assured that this resolution has not been taken without a strict regard to all the considerations appertaining to the relation which binds a dutiful citizen to his country; and that in withdrawing the tender of service, which silence in my situation might imply, I am influenced by no diminution of zeal for your future interest, no deficiency of grateful respect for your past kindness, but am supported by a full conviction that the step is compatible with both.

The acceptance of, and continuance hitherto in, the office to which your suffrages have twice called me have been a uniform sacrifice of inclination to the opinion of duty and to a deference for what appeared to be your desire. I constantly hoped that it would have been much earlier in my power, consistently with motives which I was not at liberty to disregard, to return to that retirement from which I had been reluctantly drawn. The strength of my inclination to do this, previous to the last election, had even led to the preparation of an address to declare it to you; but mature reflection on the then perplexed and critical posture of our affairs with foreign nations, and the unanimous advice of persons entitled to my confidence, impelled me to abandon the idea.

I rejoice that the state of your concerns, external as well as internal, no longer renders the pursuit of inclination incompatible with the sentiment of duty or propriety, and am persuaded, whatever partiality may be retained for my services, that, in the present circumstances of our country, you will not disapprove my determination to retire.

The impressions with which I first undertook the arduous trust were explained on the proper occasion. In the discharge of this trust, I will only say that I have, with good intentions, contributed towards the organization and administration of the government the best exertions of which a very fallible judgment was capable. Not unconscious in the outset of the inferiority of my qualifications, experience in my own eyes, perhaps still more in the eyes of others, has strengthened the motives to diffidence of myself; and every day the increasing weight of years admonishes me more and more that the shade of retirement is as necessary to me as it will be welcome. Satisfied that if any circumstances have given peculiar value to my services, they were temporary, I have the consolation to believe that, while choice and prudence invite me to quit the political scene, patriotism does not forbid it.

In looking forward to the moment which is intended to terminate the career of my public life, my feelings do not permit me to suspend the deep acknowledgment of that debt of gratitude which I owe to my beloved country for the many honors it has conferred upon me; still more for the steadfast confidence with which it has supported me; and for the opportunities I have thence enjoyed of manifesting my inviolable attachment, by services faithful and persevering, though in usefulness unequal to my zeal. If benefits have resulted to our country from these services, let it always be remembered to your praise, and as an instructive example in our annals, that under circumstances in which the passions, agitated in every direction, were liable to mislead, amidst appearances sometimes dubious, vicissitudes of fortune often discouraging, in situations in which not unfrequently want of success has countenanced the spirit of criticism, the constancy of your support was the essential prop of the efforts, and a guarantee of the plans by which they were effected. Profoundly penetrated with this idea, I shall carry it with me to my grave, as a strong incitement to unceasing vows that heaven may continue to you the choicest tokens of its beneficence; that your union and brotherly affection may be perpetual; that the free Constitution, which is the work of your hands, may be sacredly maintained; that its administration in every department may be stamped with wisdom and virtue; that, in fine, the happiness of the people of these States, under the auspices of liberty, may be made complete by so careful a preservation and so prudent a use of this blessing as will acquire to them the glory of recommending it to the applause, the affection, and adoption of every nation which is yet a stranger to it.

Here, perhaps, I ought to stop. But a solicitude for your welfare, which cannot end but with my life, and the apprehension of danger, natural to that solicitude, urge me, on an occasion like the present, to offer to your solemn contemplation, and to recommend to your frequent review, some sentiments which are the result of much reflection, of no inconsiderable observation, and which appear to me all-important to the permanency of your felicity as a people. These will be offered to you with more freedom, as you can only see in them the disinterested warnings of a parting friend, who can possibly have no personal motive to bias his counsel. Nor can I forget, as an encouragement to it, your indulgent reception of my sentiments on a former and not dissimilar occasion.

Interwoven as is the love of liberty with every ligament of your hearts, no recommendation of mine is necessary to fortify or confirm the attachment.

The unity of government which constitutes you one people is also now dear to you. It is justly so, for it is a main pillar in the edifice of your real independence, the support of your tranquility at home, your peace abroad; of your safety; of your prosperity; of that very liberty which you so highly prize. But as it is easy to foresee that, from different causes and from different quarters, much pains will be taken, many artifices employed to weaken in your minds the conviction of this truth; as this is the point in your political fortress against which the batteries of internal and external enemies will be most constantly and actively (though often covertly and insidiously) directed, it is of infinite moment that you should properly estimate the immense value of your national union to your collective and individual happiness; that you should cherish a cordial, habitual, and immovable attachment to it; accustoming yourselves to think and speak of it as of the palladium of your political safety and prosperity; watching for its preservation with jealous anxiety; discountenancing whatever may suggest even a suspicion that it can in any event be abandoned; and indignantly frowning upon the first dawning of every attempt to alienate any portion of our country from the rest, or to enfeeble the sacred ties which now link together the various parts.

For this you have every inducement of sympathy and interest. Citizens, by birth or choice, of a common country, that country has a right to concentrate your affections. The name of American, which belongs to you in your national capacity, must always exalt the just pride of patriotism more than any appellation derived from local discriminations. With slight shades of difference, you have the same religion, manners, habits, and political principles. You have in a common cause fought and triumphed together; the independence and liberty you possess are the work of joint counsels, and joint efforts of common dangers, sufferings, and successes.

But these considerations, however powerfully they address themselves to your sensibility, are greatly outweighed by those which apply more immediately to your interest. Here every portion of our country finds the most commanding motives for carefully guarding and preserving the union of the whole.

The North, in an unrestrained intercourse with the South, protected by the equal laws of a common government, finds in the productions of the latter great additional resources of maritime and commercial enterprise and precious materials of manufacturing industry. The South, in the same intercourse, benefiting by the agency of the North, sees its agriculture grow and its commerce expand. Turning partly into its own channels the seamen of the North, it finds its particular navigation invigorated; and, while it contributes, in different ways, to nourish and increase the general mass of the national navigation, it looks forward to the protection of a maritime strength, to which itself is unequally adapted. The East, in a like intercourse with the West, already finds, and in the progressive improvement of interior communications by land and water, will more and more find a valuable vent for the commodities which it brings from abroad, or manufactures at home. The West derives from the East supplies requisite to its growth and comfort, and, what is perhaps of still greater consequence, it must of necessity owe the secure enjoyment of indispensable outlets for its own productions to the weight, influence, and the future maritime strength of the Atlantic side of the Union, directed by an indissoluble community of interest as one nation. Any other tenure by which the West can hold this essential advantage, whether derived from its own separate strength, or from an apostate and unnatural connection with any foreign power, must be intrinsically precarious.

While, then, every part of our country thus feels an immediate and particular interest in union, all the parts combined cannot fail to find in the united mass of means and efforts greater strength, greater resource, proportionably greater security from external danger, a less frequent interruption of their peace by foreign nations; and, what is of inestimable value, they must derive from union an exemption from those broils and wars between themselves, which so frequently afflict neighboring countries not tied together by the same governments, which their own rival ships alone would be sufficient to produce, but which opposite foreign alliances, attachments, and intrigues would stimulate and embitter. Hence, likewise, they will avoid the necessity of those overgrown military establishments which, under any form of government, are inauspicious to liberty, and which are to be regarded as particularly hostile to republican liberty. In this sense it is that your union ought to be considered as a main prop of your liberty, and that the love of the one ought to endear to you the preservation of the other.

These considerations speak a persuasive language to every reflecting and virtuous mind, and exhibit the continuance of the Union as a primary object of patriotic desire. Is there a doubt whether a common government can embrace so large a sphere? Let experience solve it. To listen to mere speculation in such a case were criminal. We are authorized to hope that a proper organization of the whole with the auxiliary agency of governments for the respective subdivisions, will afford a happy issue to the experiment. It is well worth a fair and full experiment. With such powerful and obvious motives to union, affecting all parts of our country, while experience shall not have demonstrated its impracticability, there will always be reason to distrust the patriotism of those who in any quarter may endeavor to weaken its bands.

In contemplating the causes which may disturb our Union, it occurs as matter of serious concern that any ground should have been furnished for characterizing parties by geographical discriminations, Northern and Southern, Atlantic and Western; whence designing men may endeavor to excite a belief that there is a real difference of local interests and views. One of the expedients of party to acquire influence within particular districts is to misrepresent the opinions and aims of other districts. You cannot shield yourselves too much against the jealousies and heartburning's which spring from these misrepresentations; they tend to render alien to each other those who ought to be bound together by fraternal affection. The inhabitants of our Western country have lately had a useful lesson on this head; they have seen, in the negotiation by the Executive, and in the unanimous ratification by the Senate, of the treaty with Spain, and in the universal satisfaction at that event, throughout the United States, a decisive proof how unfounded were the suspicions propagated among them of a policy in the General Government and in the Atlantic States unfriendly to their interests in regard to the Mississippi; they have been witnesses to the formation of two treaties, that with Great Britain, and that with Spain, which secure to them everything they could desire, in respect to our foreign relations, towards confirming their prosperity. Will it not be their wisdom to rely for the preservation of these advantages on the Union by which they were procured ? Will they not henceforth be deaf to those advisers, if such there are, who would sever them from their brethren and connect them with aliens?

To the efficacy and permanency of your Union, a government for the whole is indispensable. No alliance, however strict, between the parts can be an adequate substitute; they must inevitably experience the infractions and interruptions which all alliances in all times have experienced. Sensible of this momentous truth, you have improved upon your first essay, by the adoption of a constitution of government better calculated than your former for an intimate union, and for the efficacious management of your common concerns. This government, the offspring of our own choice, uninfluenced and unawed, adopted upon full investigation and mature deliberation, completely free in its principles, in the distribution of its powers, uniting security with energy, and containing within itself a provision for its own amendment, has a just claim to your confidence and your support. Respect for its authority, compliance with its laws, acquiescence in its measures, are duties enjoined by the fundamental maxims of true liberty. The basis of our political systems is the right of the people to make and to alter their constitutions of government. But the <u>Constitution</u> which at any time exists, till changed by an explicit and authentic act of the whole people, is sacredly obligatory upon all. The very idea of the power and the right of the people to establish government presupposes the duty of every individual to obey the established government.

All obstructions to the execution of the laws, all combinations and associations, under whatever plausible character, with the real design to direct, control, counteract, or awe the regular deliberation and action of the constituted authorities, are destructive of this fundamental principle, and of fatal tendency. They serve to organize faction, to give it an artificial and extraordinary force; to put, in the place of the delegated will of the nation the will of a party, often a small but artful and enterprising minority of the community; and, according to the alternate triumphs of different parties, to make the public administration the mirror of the ill-concerted and incongruous projects of faction, rather than the organ of consistent and wholesome plans digested by common counsels and modified by mutual interests.

However combinations or associations of the above description may now and then answer popular ends, they are likely, in the course of time and things, to become potent engines, by which cunning, ambitious, and unprincipled men will be enabled to subvert the power of the people and to usurp for themselves the reins of government, destroying afterwards the very engines which have lifted them to unjust dominion.

Towards the preservation of your government, and the permanency of your present happy state, it is requisite, not only that you steadily discountenance irregular oppositions to its acknowledged authority, but also that you resist with care the spirit of innovation upon its principles, however specious the pretexts. One method of assault may be to effect, in the forms of the <u>Constitution</u>, alterations which will impair the energy of the system, and thus to undermine what cannot be directly overthrown. In all the changes to which you may be invited, remember that time and habit are at least as necessary to fix the true character of governments as of other human institutions; that experience is the surest standard by which to test the real tendency of the existing constitution of a country; that facility in changes, upon the credit of mere hypothesis and opinion, exposes to perpetual change, from the endless variety of hypothesis and opinion; and remember, especially, that for the efficient management of your common interests, in a country so extensive as ours, a government of as much vigor as is consistent with the perfect security of liberty is indispensable. Liberty itself will find in such a government, with powers properly distributed and adjusted, its surest guardian. It is, indeed, little else than a name, where the government is too feeble to withstand the enterprises of faction, to confine each member of the society within the limits prescribed by the laws, and to maintain all in the secure and tranquil enjoyment of the rights of person and property.

I have already intimated to you the danger of parties in the State, with particular reference to the founding of them on geographical discriminations. Let me now take a more comprehensive view, and warn you in the most solemn manner against the baneful effects of the spirit of party generally.

This spirit, unfortunately, is inseparable from our nature, having its root in the strongest passions of the human mind. It exists under different shapes in all governments, more or less stifled, controlled, or repressed; but, in those of the popular form, it is seen in its greatest rankness, and is truly their worst enemy. (14)

The alternate domination of one faction over another, sharpened by the spirit of revenge, natural to party dissension, which in different ages and countries has perpetrated the most horrid enormities, is itself a frightful despotism. (15) But this leads at length to a more formal and permanent despotism. **The disorders and miseries which result gradually incline the minds of men to seek security and repose in the absolute power of an individual; (16) and sooner or later the chief of some prevailing faction, more able or more fortunate than his competitors, turns this disposition**

to the purposes of his own elevation, (17) on the ruins of public liberty.

Without looking forward to an extremity of this kind (which nevertheless ought not to be entirely out of sight), the common and continual mischiefs of the spirit of party are sufficient to make it the interest and duty of a wise people to discourage and restrain it.

It serves always to distract the public councils and enfeeble the public administration (18). It agitates the community with ill-founded jealousies and false alarms (19), kindles the animosity of one part against another, foments occasionally riot and insurrection. (20) It opens the door to foreign influence and corruption, which finds a facilitated access to the government itself through the channels of party passions. Thus the policy and the will of one country are subjected to the policy and will of another.

There is an opinion that parties in free countries are useful checks upon the administration of the government and serve to keep alive the spirit of liberty. This within certain limits is probably true; and in governments of a monarchical cast, patriotism may look with indulgence, if not with favor, upon the spirit of party. But in those of the popular character, in governments purely elective, it is a spirit not to be encouraged. From their natural tendency, it is certain there will always be enough of that spirit for every salutary purpose. And there being constant danger of excess, the effort ought to be by force of public opinion, to mitigate and assuage it. A fire not to be quenched, it demands a uniform vigilance to prevent its bursting into a flame, lest, instead of warming, it should consume.

It is important, likewise, that the habits of thinking in a free country should inspire caution in those entrusted with its administration, to confine themselves within their respective constitutional spheres, avoiding in the exercise of the powers of one department to encroach upon another. **The spirit of encroachment tends to consolidate the powers of all the departments in one, and thus to create, whatever the form of government, a real despotism (21).** A just estimate of that love of power, and proneness to abuse it, which predominates in the human heart, is sufficient to satisfy us of the truth of this position. The necessity of reciprocal checks in the exercise of political power, by dividing and distributing it into different depositaries, and constituting each the guardian of the public weal against invasions by the others, has been evinced by experiments ancient and modern; some of them in our country and under our own eyes. To preserve them must be as necessary as to institute them. If, in the opinion of the people, the distribution or modification of the constitutional powers be in any particular wrong, let it be corrected by an amendment in the way which the <u>Constitution</u> designates. But let there be no change by usurpation; for though this, in one instance, may be the instrument of good, it is the customary weapon by which free governments are destroyed. The precedent must always greatly overbalance in permanent evil any partial or transient benefit, which the use can at any time yield.

Of all the dispositions and habits which lead to political prosperity, religion and morality are indispensable supports. In vain would that man claim the tribute of patriotism, who should labor to subvert these great pillars of human happiness, these firmest props of the duties of men and citizens. The mere politician, equally with the pious man, ought to respect and to cherish them. A volume could not trace all their connections with private and public felicity. Let it simply be asked: Where is the security for property, for reputation, for life, if the sense of religious obligation desert the oaths which are the instruments of investigation in courts of justice ? And let us with caution indulge the supposition that morality can be maintained without religion. Whatever may be conceded to the influence of refined education on minds of peculiar structure, reason and experience both forbid us to expect that national morality can prevail in exclusion of religious principle.

It is substantially true that virtue or morality is a necessary spring of popular government. The rule, indeed, extends with more or less force to every species of free government. Who that is a sincere friend to it can look with indifference upon attempts to shake the foundation of the fabric?

Promote then, as an object of primary importance, institutions for the general diffusion of knowledge. In proportion as the structure of a government gives force to public opinion, it is essential that public opinion should be enlightened.

As a very important source of strength and security, cherish public credit(66). One method of preserving it is to use it as sparingly as possible(67), avoiding occasions of expense by cultivating peace(partial 57), but remembering also that timely disbursements to prepare for danger frequently prevent much greater disbursements to repel it, **avoiding likewise the accumulation of debt, not only by shunning occasions of expense, but by vigorous exertion in time of peace to discharge the debts(68)** which unavoidable wars may have occasioned, **not ungenerously throwing upon posterity the burden which we ourselves ought to bear(69).** The execution of these maxims belongs to your representatives, but it is necessary that public opinion should co-operate. To facilitate to them the performance of their duty, **it is essential that you should practically bear in mind that towards the payment of debts there must be revenue(70);** that **to have revenue there must be taxes; that no taxes can be devised which are not more or less inconvenient and unpleasant; that the intrinsic embarrassment, inseparable from the selection of the proper objects (which is always a choice of difficulties), ought to be a decisive motive for a candid construction of the conduct of the government in making it, and for a spirit of acquiescence in the measures for obtaining revenue, which the public exigencies may at any time dictate.(71)**

Observe good faith and justice towards all nations; cultivate peace and harmony with all (38). Religion and morality enjoin this conduct; and can it be, that good policy does not equally enjoin it - It will be worthy of a free, enlightened, and at no distant period, a great nation, to give to mankind the magnanimous and too novel example of a people always guided by an exalted justice and benevolence. Who can doubt that, in the course of time and things, the fruits of such a plan would richly repay any temporary advantages which might be lost by a steady adherence to it ? Can it be that Providence has not connected the permanent felicity of a nation with its virtue ? The experiment, at least, is recommended by every sentiment which ennobles human nature. Alas! is it rendered impossible by its vices?

In the execution of such a plan, **nothing is more essential than that permanent, inveterate antipathies against particular nations, and passionate attachments for others (39)**, should be excluded; and that, **in place of them, just and amicable feelings towards all should be cultivated. (40) The nation which indulges towards another a habitual hatred or a habitual fondness is in some degree a slave (41).** It is a slave to its animosity or to its affection, either of which is sufficient to lead it astray from its duty and its interest. Antipathy in one nation against another disposes each more readily to offer insult and injury, to lay hold of slight causes of umbrage, and to be haughty and intractable, when accidental or trifling occasions of dispute occur. Hence, frequent collisions, obstinate, envenomed, and bloody contests. The nation, prompted by ill-will and resentment, sometimes impels to war the government, contrary to the best calculations of policy. The government sometimes participates in the national propensity and adopts through passion what reason would reject; at other times it makes the animosity of the nation subservient to projects of hostility instigated by pride, ambition, and other sinister and pernicious motives. The peace often, sometimes perhaps the liberty, of nations, has been the victim.

So likewise, **a passionate attachment of one nation for another produces a variety of evils. Sympathy for the favorite nation, facilitating the illusion of an imaginary common interest in cases where no real common interest exists, and infusing into one the enmities of the other, betrays the former into a participation in the quarrels and wars of the latter without adequate inducement or justification (42).** It leads also to **concessions to the favorite nation of privileges denied to others which is apt doubly to injure the nation making the concessions; by unnecessarily parting with what ought to have been retained, and by exciting jealousy, ill-will, and a disposition to retaliate (43),** in the parties from whom equal privileges are withheld. **And it gives to ambitious, corrupted, or deluded**

citizens (who devote themselves to the favorite nation), facility to betray or sacrifice the interests of their own country, without odium, sometimes even with popularity; gilding, with the appearances of a virtuous sense of obligation, a commendable deference for public opinion, or a laudable zeal for public good, the base or foolish compliances of ambition, corruption, or infatuation(44).

As avenues to foreign influence in innumerable ways, such attachments are particularly alarming to the truly enlightened and independent patriot. How many opportunities do they afford to tamper with domestic factions, to practice the arts of seduction, to mislead public opinion, to influence or awe the public councils. Such an attachment of a small or weak towards a great and powerful nation dooms the former to be the satellite of the latter.

Against the insidious wiles of foreign influence (I conjure you to believe me, fellow-citizens) the jealousy of a free people ought to be constantly awake, since history and experience prove that foreign influence is one of the most baneful foes of republican government. But that jealousy to be useful must be impartial; else it becomes the instrument of the very influence to be avoided, instead of a defense against it. **Excessive partiality for one foreign nation and excessive dislike of another cause those whom they actuate to see danger only on one side, and serve to veil and even second the arts of influence on the other(46)** Real patriots who may resist the intrigues of the favorite are liable to become suspected and odious, while its tools and dupes usurp the applause and confidence of the people, to surrender their interests.

The great rule of conduct for us in regard to foreign nations is in extending our commercial relations, to have with them as little political connection as possible(45). So far as we have already formed engagements, let them be fulfilled with perfect good faith. Here let us stop. Europe has a set of primary interests which to us have none; or a very remote relation. Hence she must be engaged in frequent controversies, the causes of which are essentially foreign to our concerns. Hence, therefore, it must be unwise in us to implicate ourselves by artificial ties in the ordinary vicissitudes of her politics, or the ordinary combinations and collisions of her friendships or enmities.

Our detached and distant situation invites and enables us to pursue a different course. If we remain one people under an efficient government. the period is not far off when we may defy material injury from external annoyance; **when we may take such an attitude as will cause the neutrality we may at any time resolve upon to be scrupulously respected; when belligerent nations, under the impossibility of making acquisitions upon us, will not lightly hazard the giving us provocation(47)**; when we may choose peace or war, as our interest, guided by justice, shall counsel.

Why forego the advantages of so peculiar a situation? Why quit our own to stand upon foreign ground?(56) Why, by interweaving our destiny with that of any part of Europe, entangle our peace and prosperity in the toils of European ambition, rivalship, interest, humor or caprice?(58)

It is our true policy to steer clear of permanent alliances with any portion of the foreign world(59); so far, I mean, as we are now at liberty to do it; for let me not be understood as capable of patronizing infidelity to existing engagements. **I hold the maxim no less applicable to public than to private affairs, that honesty is always the best policy(72).** I repeat it, therefore, **let those engagements be observed in their genuine sense. But, in my opinion, it is unnecessary and would be unwise to extend them(50)**

Taking care always to keep ourselves by suitable establishments on a respectable defensive posture, we may safely trust to temporary alliances for extraordinary emergencies(48).

Harmony, liberal intercourse with all nations, are recommended by policy, humanity, and interest.(51 and partial 57) But even **our commercial policy should hold an equal and impartial hand; neither seeking nor granting exclusive favors or preferences(52)**; consulting the natural course of things; **diffusing and diversifying by gentle means the streams of commerce, but forcing nothing(53); establishing (with powers so disposed, in order to give trade a stable course, to define the rights of our**

merchants, and to enable the government to support them) conventional rules of intercourse(54), the best that present circumstances and mutual opinion will permit, but temporary, and liable to be from time to time abandoned or varied, as experience and circumstances shall dictate; constantly keeping in view that **it is folly in one nation to look for disinterested favors from another; that it must pay with a portion of its independence(55)** for whatever it may accept under that character; that, by such acceptance, it may place itself in the condition of having given equivalents for nominal favors, and yet of being reproached with ingratitude for not giving more. **There can be no greater error than to expect or calculate upon real favors from nation to nation. It is an illusion, which experience must cure, which a just pride ought to discard(49).**

In offering to you, my countrymen, these counsels of an old and affectionate friend, I dare not hope they will make the strong and lasting impression I could wish; that they will control the usual current of the passions, or prevent our nation from running the course which has hitherto marked the destiny of nations. But, if I may even flatter myself that they may be productive of some partial benefit, some occasional good; that they may now and then recur to moderate the fury of party spirit, to warn against the mischiefs of foreign intrigue, to guard against the impostures of pretended patriotism; this hope will be a full recompense for the solicitude for your welfare, by which they have been dictated.

How far in the discharge of my official duties I have been guided by the principles which have been delineated, the public records and other evidences of my conduct must witness to you and to the world. To myself, the assurance of my own conscience is, that I have at least believed myself to be guided by them.

In relation to the still subsisting war in Europe, my proclamation of the twenty-second of April, 1793, is the index of my plan. Sanctioned by your approving voice, and by that of your representatives in both houses of Congress, the spirit of that measure has continually governed me, uninfluenced by any attempts to deter or divert me from it.

After deliberate examination, with the aid of the best lights I could obtain, I was well satisfied that our country, under all the circumstances of the case, had a right to take, and was bound in duty and interest to take, a neutral position. Having taken it, I determined, as far as should depend upon me, to maintain it, with moderation, perseverance, and firmness.

The considerations which respect the right to hold this conduct, it is not necessary on this occasion to detail. I will only observe that, according to my understanding of the matter, that right, so far from being denied by any of the belligerent powers, has been virtually admitted by all.

The duty of holding a neutral conduct may be inferred, without anything more, from the obligation which justice and humanity impose on every nation, in cases in which it is free to act, to maintain inviolate the relations of peace and amity towards other nations.

The inducements of interest for observing that conduct will best be referred to your own reflections and experience. With me a predominant motive has been to endeavor to gain time to our country to settle and mature its yet recent institutions, and to progress without interruption to that degree of strength and consistency which is necessary to give it, humanly speaking, the command of its own fortunes.

Though, in reviewing the incidents of my administration, I am unconscious of intentional error, I am nevertheless too sensible of my defects not to think it probable that I may have committed many errors. Whatever they may be, I fervently beseech the Almighty to avert or mitigate the evils to which they may tend. I shall also carry with me the hope that my country will never cease to view them with indulgence; and that, after forty five years of my life dedicated to its service with an upright zeal, the faults of incompetent abilities will be consigned to oblivion, as myself must soon be to the mansions of rest.

Relying on its kindness in this as in other things, and actuated by that fervent love towards it, which is so natural to a man who views in it the native soil of himself and his progenitors for several generations, I anticipate with pleasing expectation that retreat in which I promise myself to realize, without alloy, the sweet enjoyment of partaking, in the midst of my fellow-citizens, the benign influence of good laws under a free government, the ever-favorite object of my heart, and the happy reward, as I trust, of our mutual cares, labors, and dangers.

POLICY PROPOSAL INDEX

AMONG THE 95 THESES PRESENTED, only 40 are policy proposals that warrant thorough discussion and deliberation. Some of these proposals may appear radical to those unfamiliar with how the United States government was originally created and how it has been altered over the past two hundred years. It is imperative we encourage thorough and open discussion and deliberation on how to constitutionally implement these proposals.

Presented below are those 40 theses, prioritized top to bottom based on my sense of urgency balanced with the time required to garner informed public support.

Thesis 22: A candidate for political office can only accept campaign funds from individual citizens qualified to vote for them. Pg. 25

Thesis 25: Elected members of Congress must not partake in a retirement plan. They should receive Social Security like the rest of us. Pg. 32

Thesis 61: The president cannot send military troops into harm's way inside the domain of a foreign nation without a formal declaration of war by Congress. Pg. 93

Thesis 23: A candidate for political office should be limited to how many years they can serve to ensure the public benefit is not compromised by the power accumulated for their self-benefit. Pg. 28

Thesis 65: Our nation's foreign policy initiatives must never be determined by profit-driven corporations. Pg. 101

Thesis 28: End the practice of omnibus bills: any bill must pertain to one subject only, and that subject should be in the title. Pg. 36

Thesis 34: No elected official can leave elected office and work in any "position of influence" (Board of Trustees or be employed as a lobbyist) with a 501c4 for a period equal to his/her time in office. Pg. 45

Thesis 73: Create a time-definable plan to pay off the majority percentage of the debt of the federal government. Pg. 115

Thesis 77: Any federal income tax created for a specific war debt expires once those war debts are paid for. Pg. 119

Thesis 89: Establishment of, and rigid enforcement of, antitrust laws in both the state and national marketplace with a prioritized focus on media and medical conglomerates. Pg. 138

Thesis 62: The USA is to honor all obligations that have been signed, but to seek in all future relations a status of neutrality. Pg. 95

Thesis 95: Prohibit any candidate or holder of federal or state elected office, or, any person who holds a regulatory position with state or federal government, from investing in publicly held corporations. Pg. 157

Thesis 24: The source of income received by political candidates or office holders must be fully disclosed. Pg. 31

Thesis 90: The federal government should be prohibited to intervene in an individual's right to self-medicate. Pg. 143

Thesis 93: Prohibit local/state/federal administrative support for political party primaries. Pg. 151

Thesis 94: Prohibit any person holding federal position (elected or employee) from joining the board of a corporation or being hired as executive leadership in a corporation for a time period equal to their most recent time in office/employment. Pg. 153

Thesis 87: Constitutional amendment to distinguish natural persons, or individual citizens, from artificial personas, or corporations.